THIS IS YOUR **PASSBOOK**® FOR ...

STAFF ANALYST

NATIONAL LEARNING CORPORATION®

passbooks.com

PASSBOOK® SERIES

THE *PASSBOOK® SERIES* has been created to prepare applicants and candidates for the ultimate academic battlefield – the examination room.

At some time in our lives, each and every one of us may be required to take an examination – for validation, matriculation, admission, qualification, registration, certification, or licensure.

Based on the assumption that every applicant or candidate has met the basic formal educational standards, has taken the required number of courses, and read the necessary texts, the *PASSBOOK® SERIES* furnishes the one special preparation which may assure passing with confidence, instead of failing with insecurity. Examination questions – together with answers – are furnished as the basic vehicle for study so that the mysteries of the examination and its compounding difficulties may be eliminated or diminished by a sure method.

This book is meant to help you pass your examination provided that you qualify and are serious in your objective.

The entire field is reviewed through the huge store of content information which is succinctly presented through a provocative and challenging approach – the question-and-answer method.

A climate of success is established by furnishing the correct answers at the end of each test.

You soon learn to recognize types of questions, forms of questions, and patterns of questioning. You may even begin to anticipate expected outcomes.

You perceive that many questions are repeated or adapted so that you can gain acute insights, which may enable you to score many sure points.

You learn how to confront new questions, or types of questions, and to attack them confidently and work out the correct answers.

You note objectives and emphases, and recognize pitfalls and dangers, so that you may make positive educational adjustments.

Moreover, you are kept fully informed in relation to new concepts, methods, practices, and directions in the field.

You discover that you arre actually taking the examination all the time: you are preparing for the examination by "taking" an examination, not by reading extraneous and/or supererogatory textbooks.

In short, this PASSBOOK®, used directedly, should be an important factor in helping you to pass your test.

STAFF ANALYST

DUTIES AND RESPONSIBILITIES

Under direct supervision, performs technical work in personnel management and in public employee labor relations; professional work of ordinary technical difficulty and responsibility, assisting in the preparation and conduct of management surveys, maintenance of budgetary controls, administrative and procedural analyses, and the evaluation of organizational structures, policies, programs, projects, practices, and operations or city agencies, and compliance with provisions of a contract between a private agency and an agency of the city; may utilize quantitative analysis and cost accounting techniques; performs related work.

EXAMPLES OF TYPICAL TASKS

Assists in the conduct of job analyses, personnel testing classification, and employee development activities, including safety programs, and in employee benefit programs; assists in the planning and coordinating of agency activities in personnel administration and labor relations; assists in collective bargaining negotiations, mediation, impasse, grievance and other proceedings, provides research support, assists in conduct of wage and fringe benefit surveys and contract administration; assists in the conduct of management surveys and studies, collects and analyzes data on the operations of city agencies, or to determine compliance with the provisions of a contract between a private organization and a city agency, including budgetary requirements; analyzes organizational structures, operational and accounting systems, including data processing methods, procedures, programs, systems, manpower requirements, utilization of machines and equipment, space layouts, forms design, records management, performance standards, personnel administration, and other aspects of management to achieve greater organizational efficiency; assists in installing methods, systems, forms or procedures; assists in the preparation of comprehensive reports of findings with recommendations for improved efficiency; assists in the preparation of periodic reports on departmental programs; assists in the preparation, maintenance, and revision of systems and procedure manuals and designs forms; assists in the preparation of charts, graphs, and other related material; assists in the discussion of recommended proposals with the agency heads and in the installation of accepted proposals.

TESTS

The written test will be of the multiple-choice type and may involve questions concerning, and the ability to analyze problems in, the following areas: job analysis; budget planning and analysis; management and methods; organization and structures; policy programming, planning, and evaluation; space utilization and other pertinent fields. It may also include questions on the following: principles, methods, and techniques in all aspects of personnel administration which are included in the typical tasks for this title; budgeting; municipal labor relations; management; policy program and project analysis as well as questions on administrative techniques; research techniques applicable to the duties indicated for the typical tasks, including quantitative analysis techniques; computer utilization; statistics and date collection techniques; comprehension and interpretation of pertinent written material including technical data report writing techniques including English usage; cost analysis and cost accounting; public and employee relations and other related areas.

HOW TO TAKE A TEST

I. YOU MUST PASS AN EXAMINATION

A. *WHAT EVERY CANDIDATE SHOULD KNOW*

Examination applicants often ask us for help in preparing for the written test. What can I study in advance? What kinds of questions will be asked? How will the test be given? How will the papers be graded?

As an applicant for a civil service examination, you may be wondering about some of these things. Our purpose here is to suggest effective methods of advance study and to describe civil service examinations.

Your chances for success on this examination can be increased if you know how to prepare. Those "pre-examination jitters" can be reduced if you know what to expect. You can even experience an adventure in good citizenship if you know why civil service exams are given.

B. *WHY ARE CIVIL SERVICE EXAMINATIONS GIVEN?*

Civil service examinations are important to you in two ways. As a citizen, you want public jobs filled by employees who know how to do their work. As a job seeker, you want a fair chance to compete for that job on an equal footing with other candidates. The best-known means of accomplishing this two-fold goal is the competitive examination.

Exams are widely publicized throughout the nation. They may be administered for jobs in federal, state, city, municipal, town or village governments or agencies.

Any citizen may apply, with some limitations, such as the age or residence of applicants. Your experience and education may be reviewed to see whether you meet the requirements for the particular examination. When these requirements exist, they are reasonable and applied consistently to all applicants. Thus, a competitive examination may cause you some uneasiness now, but it is your privilege and safeguard.

C. *HOW ARE CIVIL SERVICE EXAMS DEVELOPED?*

Examinations are carefully written by trained technicians who are specialists in the field known as "psychological measurement," in consultation with recognized authorities in the field of work that the test will cover. These experts recommend the subject matter areas or skills to be tested; only those knowledges or skills important to your success on the job are included. The most reliable books and source materials available are used as references. Together, the experts and technicians judge the difficulty level of the questions.

Test technicians know how to phrase questions so that the problem is clearly stated. Their ethics do not permit "trick" or "catch" questions. Questions may have been tried out on sample groups, or subjected to statistical analysis, to determine their usefulness.

Written tests are often used in combination with performance tests, ratings of training and experience, and oral interviews. All of these measures combine to form the best-known means of finding the right person for the right job.

II. HOW TO PASS THE WRITTEN TEST

A. NATURE OF THE EXAMINATION

To prepare intelligently for civil service examinations, you should know how they differ from school examinations you have taken. In school you were assigned certain definite pages to read or subjects to cover. The examination questions were quite detailed and usually emphasized memory. Civil service exams, on the other hand, try to discover your present ability to perform the duties of a position, plus your potentiality to learn these duties. In other words, a civil service exam attempts to predict how successful you will be. Questions cover such a broad area that they cannot be as minute and detailed as school exam questions.

In the public service similar kinds of work, or positions, are grouped together in one "class." This process is known as *position-classification*. All the positions in a class are paid according to the salary range for that class. One class title covers all of these positions, and they are all tested by the same examination.

B. FOUR BASIC STEPS

1) Study the announcement

How, then, can you know what subjects to study? Our best answer is: "Learn as much as possible about the class of positions for which you've applied." The exam will test the knowledge, skills and abilities needed to do the work.

Your most valuable source of information about the position you want is the official exam announcement. This announcement lists the training and experience qualifications. Check these standards and apply only if you come reasonably close to meeting them.

The brief description of the position in the examination announcement offers some clues to the subjects which will be tested. Think about the job itself. Review the duties in your mind. Can you perform them, or are there some in which you are rusty? Fill in the blank spots in your preparation.

Many jurisdictions preview the written test in the exam announcement by including a section called "Knowledge and Abilities Required," "Scope of the Examination," or some similar heading. Here you will find out specifically what fields will be tested.

2) Review your own background

Once you learn in general what the position is all about, and what you need to know to do the work, ask yourself which subjects you already know fairly well and which need improvement. You may wonder whether to concentrate on improving your strong areas or on building some background in your fields of weakness. When the announcement has specified "some knowledge" or "considerable knowledge," or has used adjectives like "beginning principles of..." or "advanced ... methods," you can get a clue as to the number and difficulty of questions to be asked in any given field. More questions, and hence broader coverage, would be included for those subjects which are more important in the work. Now weigh your strengths and weaknesses against the job requirements and prepare accordingly.

3) Determine the level of the position

Another way to tell how intensively you should prepare is to understand the level of the job for which you are applying. Is it the entering level? In other words, is this the position in which beginners in a field of work are hired? Or is it an intermediate or advanced level? Sometimes this is indicated by such words as "Junior" or "Senior" in the class title. Other jurisdictions use Roman numerals to designate the level – Clerk I, Clerk II, for example. The word "Supervisor" sometimes appears in the title. If the level is not indicated by the title, check the description of duties. Will you be working under very close supervision, or will you have responsibility for independent decisions in this work?

4) Choose appropriate study materials

Now that you know the subjects to be examined and the relative amount of each subject to be covered, you can choose suitable study materials. For beginning level jobs, or even advanced ones, if you have a pronounced weakness in some aspect of your training, read a modern, standard textbook in that field. Be sure it is up to date and has general coverage. Such books are normally available at your library, and the librarian will be glad to help you locate one. For entry-level positions, questions of appropriate difficulty are chosen – neither highly advanced questions, nor those too simple. Such questions require careful thought but not advanced training.

If the position for which you are applying is technical or advanced, you will read more advanced, specialized material. If you are already familiar with the basic principles of your field, elementary textbooks would waste your time. Concentrate on advanced textbooks and technical periodicals. Think through the concepts and review difficult problems in your field.

These are all general sources. You can get more ideas on your own initiative, following these leads. For example, training manuals and publications of the government agency which employs workers in your field can be useful, particularly for technical and professional positions. A letter or visit to the government department involved may result in more specific study suggestions, and certainly will provide you with a more definite idea of the exact nature of the position you are seeking.

III. KINDS OF TESTS

Tests are used for purposes other than measuring knowledge and ability to perform specified duties. For some positions, it is equally important to test ability to make adjustments to new situations or to profit from training. In others, basic mental abilities not dependent on information are essential. Questions which test these things may not appear as pertinent to the duties of the position as those which test for knowledge and information. Yet they are often highly important parts of a fair examination. For very general questions, it is almost impossible to help you direct your study efforts. What we can do is to point out some of the more common of these general abilities needed in public service positions and describe some typical questions.

1) General information

Broad, general information has been found useful for predicting job success in some kinds of work. This is tested in a variety of ways, from vocabulary lists to questions about current events. Basic background in some field of work, such as sociology or economics, may be sampled in a group of questions. Often these are principles which have become familiar to most persons through exposure rather than through formal training. It is difficult to advise you how to study for these questions; being alert to the world around you is our best suggestion.

2) Verbal ability

An example of an ability needed in many positions is verbal or language ability. Verbal ability is, in brief, the ability to use and understand words. Vocabulary and grammar tests are typical measures of this ability. Reading comprehension or paragraph interpretation questions are common in many kinds of civil service tests. You are given a paragraph of written material and asked to find its central meaning.

3) Numerical ability

Number skills can be tested by the familiar arithmetic problem, by checking paired lists of numbers to see which are alike and which are different, or by interpreting charts and graphs. In the latter test, a graph may be printed in the test booklet which you are asked to use as the basis for answering questions.

4) Observation

A popular test for law-enforcement positions is the observation test. A picture is shown to you for several minutes, then taken away. Questions about the picture test your ability to observe both details and larger elements.

5) Following directions

In many positions in the public service, the employee must be able to carry out written instructions dependably and accurately. You may be given a chart with several columns, each column listing a variety of information. The questions require you to carry out directions involving the information given in the chart.

6) Skills and aptitudes

Performance tests effectively measure some manual skills and aptitudes. When the skill is one in which you are trained, such as typing or shorthand, you can practice. These tests are often very much like those given in business school or high school courses. For many of the other skills and aptitudes, however, no short-time preparation can be made. Skills and abilities natural to you or that you have developed throughout your lifetime are being tested.

Many of the general questions just described provide all the data needed to answer the questions and ask you to use your reasoning ability to find the answers. Your best preparation for these tests, as well as for tests of facts and ideas, is to be at your physical and mental best. You, no doubt, have your own methods of getting into an exam-taking mood and keeping "in shape." The next section lists some ideas on this subject.

IV. KINDS OF QUESTIONS

Only rarely is the "essay" question, which you answer in narrative form, used in civil service tests. Civil service tests are usually of the short-answer type. Full instructions for answering these questions will be given to you at the examination. But in case this is your first experience with short-answer questions and separate answer sheets, here is what you need to know:

1) Multiple-choice Questions

Most popular of the short-answer questions is the "multiple choice" or "best answer" question. It can be used, for example, to test for factual knowledge, ability to solve problems or judgment in meeting situations found at work.

A multiple-choice question is normally one of three types—

- It can begin with an incomplete statement followed by several possible endings. You are to find the one ending which *best* completes the statement, although some of the others may not be entirely wrong.
- It can also be a complete statement in the form of a question which is answered by choosing one of the statements listed.
- It can be in the form of a problem – again you select the best answer.

Here is an example of a multiple-choice question with a discussion which should give you some clues as to the method for choosing the right answer:

When an employee has a complaint about his assignment, the action which will *best* help him overcome his difficulty is to
- A. discuss his difficulty with his coworkers
- B. take the problem to the head of the organization
- C. take the problem to the person who gave him the assignment
- D. say nothing to anyone about his complaint

In answering this question, you should study each of the choices to find which is best. Consider choice "A" – Certainly an employee may discuss his complaint with fellow employees, but no change or improvement can result, and the complaint remains unresolved. Choice "B" is a poor choice since the head of the organization probably does not know what assignment you have been given, and taking your problem to him is known as "going over the head" of the supervisor. The supervisor, or person who made the assignment, is the person who can clarify it or correct any injustice. Choice "C" is, therefore, correct. To say nothing, as in choice "D," is unwise. Supervisors have and interest in knowing the problems employees are facing, and the employee is seeking a solution to his problem.

2) True/False Questions

The "true/false" or "right/wrong" form of question is sometimes used. Here a complete statement is given. Your job is to decide whether the statement is right or wrong.

SAMPLE: A roaming cell-phone call to a nearby city costs less than a non-roaming call to a distant city.

This statement is wrong, or false, since roaming calls are more expensive.

This is not a complete list of all possible question forms, although most of the others are variations of these common types. You will always get complete directions for answering questions. Be sure you understand *how* to mark your answers – ask questions until you do.

V. RECORDING YOUR ANSWERS

Computer terminals are used more and more today for many different kinds of exams.

For an examination with very few applicants, you may be told to record your answers in the test booklet itself. Separate answer sheets are much more common. If this separate answer sheet is to be scored by machine – and this is often the case – it is highly important that you mark your answers correctly in order to get credit.

An electronic scoring machine is often used in civil service offices because of the speed with which papers can be scored. Machine-scored answer sheets must be marked with a pencil, which will be given to you. This pencil has a high graphite content which responds to the electronic scoring machine. As a matter of fact, stray dots may register as answers, so do not let your pencil rest on the answer sheet while you are pondering the correct answer. Also, if your pencil lead breaks or is otherwise defective, ask for another.

Since the answer sheet will be dropped in a slot in the scoring machine, be careful not to bend the corners or get the paper crumpled.

The answer sheet normally has five vertical columns of numbers, with 30 numbers to a column. These numbers correspond to the question numbers in your test booklet. After each number, going across the page are four or five pairs of dotted lines. These short dotted lines have small letters or numbers above them. The first two pairs may also have a "T" or "F" above the letters. This indicates that the first two pairs only are to be used if the questions are of the true-false type. If the questions are multiple choice, disregard the "T" and "F" and pay attention only to the small letters or numbers.

Answer your questions in the manner of the sample that follows:

32. The largest city in the United States is
    A. Washington, D.C.
    B. New York City
    C. Chicago
    D. Detroit
    E. San Francisco

1) Choose the answer you think is best. (New York City is the largest, so "B" is correct.)
2) Find the row of dotted lines numbered the same as the question you are answering. (Find row number 32)
3) Find the pair of dotted lines corresponding to the answer. (Find the pair of lines under the mark "B.")
4) Make a solid black mark between the dotted lines.

VI. BEFORE THE TEST

Common sense will help you find procedures to follow to get ready for an examination. Too many of us, however, overlook these sensible measures. Indeed, nervousness and fatigue have been found to be the most serious reasons why applicants fail to do their best on civil service tests. Here is a list of reminders:

- Begin your preparation early – Don't wait until the last minute to go scurrying around for books and materials or to find out what the position is all about.
- Prepare continuously – An hour a night for a week is better than an all-night cram session. This has been definitely established. What is more, a night a week for a month will return better dividends than crowding your study into a shorter period of time.
- Locate the place of the exam – You have been sent a notice telling you when and where to report for the examination. If the location is in a different town or otherwise unfamiliar to you, it would be well to inquire the best route and learn something about the building.
- Relax the night before the test – Allow your mind to rest. Do not study at all that night. Plan some mild recreation or diversion; then go to bed early and get a good night's sleep.
- Get up early enough to make a leisurely trip to the place for the test – This way unforeseen events, traffic snarls, unfamiliar buildings, etc. will not upset you.
- Dress comfortably – A written test is not a fashion show. You will be known by number and not by name, so wear something comfortable.
- Leave excess paraphernalia at home – Shopping bags and odd bundles will get in your way. You need bring only the items mentioned in the official notice you received; usually everything you need is provided. Do not bring reference books to the exam. They will only confuse those last minutes and be taken away from you when in the test room.
- Arrive somewhat ahead of time – If because of transportation schedules you must get there very early, bring a newspaper or magazine to take your mind off yourself while waiting.
- Locate the examination room – When you have found the proper room, you will be directed to the seat or part of the room where you will sit. Sometimes you are given a sheet of instructions to read while you are waiting. Do not fill out any forms until you are told to do so; just read them and be prepared.
- Relax and prepare to listen to the instructions
- If you have any physical problem that may keep you from doing your best, be sure to tell the test administrator. If you are sick or in poor health, you really cannot do your best on the exam. You can come back and take the test some other time.

VII. AT THE TEST

The day of the test is here and you have the test booklet in your hand. The temptation to get going is very strong. Caution! There is more to success than knowing the right answers. You must know how to identify your papers and understand variations in the type of short-answer question used in this particular examination. Follow these suggestions for maximum results from your efforts:

1) Cooperate with the monitor

The test administrator has a duty to create a situation in which you can be as much at ease as possible. He will give instructions, tell you when to begin, check to see that you are marking your answer sheet correctly, and so on. He is not there to guard you, although he will see that your competitors do not take unfair advantage. He wants to help you do your best.

2) Listen to all instructions

Don't jump the gun! Wait until you understand all directions. In most civil service tests you get more time than you need to answer the questions. So don't be in a hurry. Read each word of instructions until you clearly understand the meaning. Study the examples, listen to all announcements and follow directions. Ask questions if you do not understand what to do.

3) Identify your papers

Civil service exams are usually identified by number only. You will be assigned a number; you must not put your name on your test papers. Be sure to copy your number correctly. Since more than one exam may be given, copy your exact examination title.

4) Plan your time

Unless you are told that a test is a "speed" or "rate of work" test, speed itself is usually not important. Time enough to answer all the questions will be provided, but this does not mean that you have all day. An overall time limit has been set. Divide the total time (in minutes) by the number of questions to determine the approximate time you have for each question.

5) Do not linger over difficult questions

If you come across a difficult question, mark it with a paper clip (useful to have along) and come back to it when you have been through the booklet. One caution if you do this – be sure to skip a number on your answer sheet as well. Check often to be sure that you have not lost your place and that you are marking in the row numbered the same as the question you are answering.

6) Read the questions

Be sure you know what the question asks! Many capable people are unsuccessful because they failed to *read* the questions correctly.

7) Answer all questions

Unless you have been instructed that a penalty will be deducted for incorrect answers, it is better to guess than to omit a question.

8) Speed tests

It is often better NOT to guess on speed tests. It has been found that on timed tests people are tempted to spend the last few seconds before time is called in marking answers at random – without even reading them – in the hope of picking up a few extra points. To discourage this practice, the instructions may warn you that your score will be "corrected" for guessing. That is, a penalty will be applied. The incorrect answers will be deducted from the correct ones, or some other penalty formula will be used.

9) Review your answers

If you finish before time is called, go back to the questions you guessed or omitted to give them further thought. Review other answers if you have time.

10) Return your test materials

If you are ready to leave before others have finished or time is called, take ALL your materials to the monitor and leave quietly. Never take any test material with you. The monitor can discover whose papers are not complete, and taking a test booklet may be grounds for disqualification.

VIII. EXAMINATION TECHNIQUES

1) Read the general instructions carefully. These are usually printed on the first page of the exam booklet. As a rule, these instructions refer to the timing of the examination; the fact that you should not start work until the signal and must stop work at a signal, etc. If there are any *special* instructions, such as a choice of questions to be answered, make sure that you note this instruction carefully.

2) When you are ready to start work on the examination, that is as soon as the signal has been given, read the instructions to each question booklet, underline any key words or phrases, such as *least, best, outline, describe* and the like. In this way you will tend to answer as requested rather than discover on reviewing your paper that you *listed without describing*, that you selected the *worst* choice rather than the *best* choice, etc.

3) If the examination is of the objective or multiple-choice type – that is, each question will also give a series of possible answers: A, B, C or D, and you are called upon to select the best answer and write the letter next to that answer on your answer paper – it is advisable to start answering each question in turn. There may be anywhere from 50 to 100 such questions in the three or four hours allotted and you can see how much time would be taken if you read through all the questions before beginning to answer any. Furthermore, if you come across a question or group of questions which you know would be difficult to answer, it would undoubtedly affect your handling of all the other questions.

4) If the examination is of the essay type and contains but a few questions, it is a moot point as to whether you should read all the questions before starting to answer any one. Of course, if you are given a choice – say five out of seven and the like – then it is essential to read all the questions so you can eliminate the two that are most difficult. If, however, you are asked to answer all the questions, there may be danger in trying to answer the easiest one first because you may find that you will spend too much time on it. The best technique is to answer the first question, then proceed to the second, etc.

5) Time your answers. Before the exam begins, write down the time it started, then add the time allowed for the examination and write down the time it must be completed, then divide the time available somewhat as follows:

- If 3-1/2 hours are allowed, that would be 210 minutes. If you have 80 objective-type questions, that would be an average of 2-1/2 minutes per question. Allow yourself no more than 2 minutes per question, or a total of 160 minutes, which will permit about 50 minutes to review.
- If for the time allotment of 210 minutes there are 7 essay questions to answer, that would average about 30 minutes a question. Give yourself only 25 minutes per question so that you have about 35 minutes to review.

6) The most important instruction is to *read each question* and make sure you know what is wanted. The second most important instruction is to *time yourself properly* so that you answer every question. The third most important instruction is to *answer every question*. Guess if you have to but include something for each question. Remember that you will receive no credit for a blank and will probably receive some credit if you write something in answer to an essay question. If you guess a letter – say "B" for a multiple-choice question – you may have guessed right. If you leave a blank as an answer to a multiple-choice question, the examiners may respect your feelings but it will not add a point to your score. Some exams may penalize you for wrong answers, so in such cases *only*, you may not want to guess unless you have some basis for your answer.

7) Suggestions
  a. Objective-type questions
    1. Examine the question booklet for proper sequence of pages and questions
    2. Read all instructions carefully
    3. Skip any question which seems too difficult; return to it after all other questions have been answered
    4. Apportion your time properly; do not spend too much time on any single question or group of questions
    5. Note and underline key words – *all, most, fewest, least, best, worst, same, opposite,* etc.
    6. Pay particular attention to negatives
    7. Note unusual option, e.g., unduly long, short, complex, different or similar in content to the body of the question
    8. Observe the use of "hedging" words – *probably, may, most likely,* etc.
    9. Make sure that your answer is put next to the same number as the question
    10. Do not second-guess unless you have good reason to believe the second answer is definitely more correct
    11. Cross out original answer if you decide another answer is more accurate; do not erase until you are ready to hand your paper in
    12. Answer all questions; guess unless instructed otherwise
    13. Leave time for review

  b. Essay questions
    1. Read each question carefully
    2. Determine exactly what is wanted. Underline key words or phrases.
    3. Decide on outline or paragraph answer

4. Include many different points and elements unless asked to develop any one or two points or elements
5. Show impartiality by giving pros and cons unless directed to select one side only
6. Make and write down any assumptions you find necessary to answer the questions
7. Watch your English, grammar, punctuation and choice of words
8. Time your answers; don't crowd material

8) Answering the essay question

Most essay questions can be answered by framing the specific response around several key words or ideas. Here are a few such key words or ideas:

M's: manpower, materials, methods, money, management
P's: purpose, program, policy, plan, procedure, practice, problems, pitfalls, personnel, public relations
   a. Six basic steps in handling problems:
      1. Preliminary plan and background development
      2. Collect information, data and facts
      3. Analyze and interpret information, data and facts
      4. Analyze and develop solutions as well as make recommendations
      5. Prepare report and sell recommendations
      6. Install recommendations and follow up effectiveness

   b. Pitfalls to avoid
      1. *Taking things for granted* – A statement of the situation does not necessarily imply that each of the elements is necessarily true; for example, a complaint may be invalid and biased so that all that can be taken for granted is that a complaint has been registered
      2. *Considering only one side of a situation* – Wherever possible, indicate several alternatives and then point out the reasons you selected the best one
      3. *Failing to indicate follow up* – Whenever your answer indicates action on your part, make certain that you will take proper follow-up action to see how successful your recommendations, procedures or actions turn out to be
      4. *Taking too long in answering any single question* – Remember to time your answers properly

IX. AFTER THE TEST

Scoring procedures differ in detail among civil service jurisdictions although the general principles are the same. Whether the papers are hand-scored or graded by machine we have described, they are nearly always graded by number. That is, the person who marks the paper knows only the number – never the name – of the applicant. Not until all the papers have been graded will they be matched with names. If other tests, such as training and experience or oral interview ratings have been given, scores will be combined. Different parts of the examination usually have different weights. For example, the written test might count 60 percent of the final grade, and a rating of training and experience 40 percent. In many jurisdictions, veterans will have a certain number of points added to their grades.

After the final grade has been determined, the names are placed in grade order and an eligible list is established. There are various methods for resolving ties between those who get the same final grade – probably the most common is to place first the name of the person whose application was received first. Job offers are made from the eligible list in the order the names appear on it. You will be notified of your grade and your rank as soon as all these computations have been made. This will be done as rapidly as possible.

People who are found to meet the requirements in the announcement are called "eligibles." Their names are put on a list of eligible candidates. An eligible's chances of getting a job depend on how high he stands on this list and how fast agencies are filling jobs from the list.

When a job is to be filled from a list of eligibles, the agency asks for the names of people on the list of eligibles for that job. When the civil service commission receives this request, it sends to the agency the names of the three people highest on this list. Or, if the job to be filled has specialized requirements, the office sends the agency the names of the top three persons who meet these requirements from the general list.

The appointing officer makes a choice from among the three people whose names were sent to him. If the selected person accepts the appointment, the names of the others are put back on the list to be considered for future openings.

That is the rule in hiring from all kinds of eligible lists, whether they are for typist, carpenter, chemist, or something else. For every vacancy, the appointing officer has his choice of any one of the top three eligibles on the list. This explains why the person whose name is on top of the list sometimes does not get an appointment when some of the persons lower on the list do. If the appointing officer chooses the second or third eligible, the No. 1 eligible does not get a job at once, but stays on the list until he is appointed or the list is terminated.

X. HOW TO PASS THE INTERVIEW TEST

The examination for which you applied requires an oral interview test. You have already taken the written test and you are now being called for the interview test – the final part of the formal examination.

You may think that it is not possible to prepare for an interview test and that there are no procedures to follow during an interview. Our purpose is to point out some things you can do in advance that will help you and some good rules to follow and pitfalls to avoid while you are being interviewed.

What is an interview supposed to test?

The written examination is designed to test the technical knowledge and competence of the candidate; the oral is designed to evaluate intangible qualities, not readily measured otherwise, and to establish a list showing the relative fitness of each candidate – as measured against his competitors – for the position sought. Scoring is not on the basis of "right" and "wrong," but on a sliding scale of values ranging from "not passable" to "outstanding." As a matter of fact, it is possible to achieve a relatively low score without a single "incorrect" answer because of evident weakness in the qualities being measured.

Occasionally, an examination may consist entirely of an oral test – either an individual or a group oral. In such cases, information is sought concerning the technical knowledges and abilities of the candidate, since there has been no written examination for this purpose. More commonly, however, an oral test is used to supplement a written examination.

Who conducts interviews?

The composition of oral boards varies among different jurisdictions. In nearly all, a representative of the personnel department serves as chairman. One of the members of the board may be a representative of the department in which the candidate would work. In some cases, "outside experts" are used, and, frequently, a businessman or some other representative of the general public is asked to serve. Labor and management or other special groups may be represented. The aim is to secure the services of experts in the appropriate field.

However the board is composed, it is a good idea (and not at all improper or unethical) to ascertain in advance of the interview who the members are and what groups they represent. When you are introduced to them, you will have some idea of their backgrounds and interests, and at least you will not stutter and stammer over their names.

What should be done before the interview?

While knowledge about the board members is useful and takes some of the surprise element out of the interview, there is other preparation which is more substantive. It *is* possible to prepare for an oral interview – in several ways:

1) Keep a copy of your application and review it carefully before the interview

This may be the only document before the oral board, and the starting point of the interview. Know what education and experience you have listed there, and the sequence and dates of all of it. Sometimes the board will ask you to review the highlights of your experience for them; you should not have to hem and haw doing it.

2) Study the class specification and the examination announcement

Usually, the oral board has one or both of these to guide them. The qualities, characteristics or knowledges required by the position sought are stated in these documents. They offer valuable clues as to the nature of the oral interview. For example, if the job involves supervisory responsibilities, the announcement will usually indicate that knowledge of modern supervisory methods and the qualifications of the candidate as a supervisor will be tested. If so, you can expect such questions, frequently in the form of a hypothetical situation which you are expected to solve. NEVER go into an oral without knowledge of the duties and responsibilities of the job you seek.

3) Think through each qualification required

Try to visualize the kind of questions you would ask if you were a board member. How well could you answer them? Try especially to appraise your own knowledge and background in each area, *measured against the job sought*, and identify any areas in which you are weak. Be critical and realistic – do not flatter yourself.

4) Do some general reading in areas in which you feel you may be weak

For example, if the job involves supervision and your past experience has NOT, some general reading in supervisory methods and practices, particularly in the field of human relations, might be useful. Do NOT study agency procedures or detailed manuals. The oral board will be testing your understanding and capacity, not your memory.

5) Get a good night's sleep and watch your general health and mental attitude

You will want a clear head at the interview. Take care of a cold or any other minor ailment, and of course, no hangovers.

What should be done on the day of the interview?

Now comes the day of the interview itself. Give yourself plenty of time to get there. Plan to arrive somewhat ahead of the scheduled time, particularly if your appointment is in the fore part of the day. If a previous candidate fails to appear, the board might be ready for you a bit early. By early afternoon an oral board is almost invariably behind schedule if there are many candidates, and you may have to wait. Take along a book or magazine to read, or your application to review, but leave any extraneous material in the waiting room when you go in for your interview. In any event, relax and compose yourself.

The matter of dress is important. The board is forming impressions about you – from your experience, your manners, your attitude, and your appearance. Give your personal appearance careful attention. Dress your best, but not your flashiest. Choose conservative, appropriate clothing, and be sure it is immaculate. This is a business interview, and your appearance should indicate that you regard it as such. Besides, being well groomed and properly dressed will help boost your confidence.

Sooner or later, someone will call your name and escort you into the interview room. *This is it.* From here on you are on your own. It is too late for any more preparation. But remember, you asked for this opportunity to prove your fitness, and you are here because your request was granted.

What happens when you go in?

The usual sequence of events will be as follows: The clerk (who is often the board stenographer) will introduce you to the chairman of the oral board, who will introduce you to the other members of the board. Acknowledge the introductions before you sit down. Do not be surprised if you find a microphone facing you or a stenotypist sitting by. Oral interviews are usually recorded in the event of an appeal or other review.

Usually the chairman of the board will open the interview by reviewing the highlights of your education and work experience from your application – primarily for the benefit of the other members of the board, as well as to get the material into the record. Do not interrupt or comment unless there is an error or significant misinterpretation; if that is the case, do not hesitate. But do not quibble about insignificant matters. Also, he will usually ask you some question about your education, experience or your present job – partly to get you to start talking and to establish the interviewing "rapport." He may start the actual questioning, or turn it over to one of the other members. Frequently, each member undertakes the questioning on a particular area, one in which he is perhaps most competent, so you can expect each member to participate in the examination. Because time is limited, you may also expect some rather abrupt switches in the direction the questioning takes, so do not be upset by it. Normally, a board member will not pursue a single line of questioning unless he discovers a particular strength or weakness.

After each member has participated, the chairman will usually ask whether any member has any further questions, then will ask you if you have anything you wish to add. Unless you are expecting this question, it may floor you. Worse, it may start you off on an extended, extemporaneous speech. The board is not usually seeking more information. The question is principally to offer you a last opportunity to present further qualifications or to indicate that you have nothing to add. So, if you feel that a significant qualification or characteristic has been overlooked, it is proper to point it out in a sentence or so. Do not compliment the board on the thoroughness of their examination – they have been sketchy, and you know it. If you wish, merely say, "No thank you, I have nothing further to add." This is a point where you can "talk yourself out" of a good impression or fail to present an important bit of information. Remember, *you close the interview yourself.*

The chairman will then say, "That is all, Mr. _____, thank you." Do not be startled; the interview is over, and quicker than you think. Thank him, gather your belongings and take your leave. Save your sigh of relief for the other side of the door.

How to put your best foot forward

Throughout this entire process, you may feel that the board individually and collectively is trying to pierce your defenses, seek out your hidden weaknesses and embarrass and confuse you. Actually, this is not true. They are obliged to make an appraisal of your qualifications for the job you are seeking, and they want to see you in your best light. Remember, they must interview all candidates and a non-cooperative candidate may become a failure in spite of their best efforts to bring out his qualifications. Here are 15 suggestions that will help you:

1) Be natural – Keep your attitude confident, not cocky

If you are not confident that you can do the job, do not expect the board to be. Do not apologize for your weaknesses, try to bring out your strong points. The board is interested in a positive, not negative, presentation. Cockiness will antagonize any board member and make him wonder if you are covering up a weakness by a false show of strength.

2) Get comfortable, but don't lounge or sprawl

Sit erectly but not stiffly. A careless posture may lead the board to conclude that you are careless in other things, or at least that you are not impressed by the importance of the occasion. Either conclusion is natural, even if incorrect. Do not fuss with your clothing, a pencil or an ashtray. Your hands may occasionally be useful to emphasize a point; do not let them become a point of distraction.

3) Do not wisecrack or make small talk

This is a serious situation, and your attitude should show that you consider it as such. Further, the time of the board is limited – they do not want to waste it, and neither should you.

4) Do not exaggerate your experience or abilities

In the first place, from information in the application or other interviews and sources, the board may know more about you than you think. Secondly, you probably will not get away with it. An experienced board is rather adept at spotting such a situation, so do not take the chance.

5) If you know a board member, do not make a point of it, yet do not hide it

Certainly you are not fooling him, and probably not the other members of the board. Do not try to take advantage of your acquaintanceship – it will probably do you little good.

6) Do not dominate the interview

Let the board do that. They will give you the clues – do not assume that you have to do all the talking. Realize that the board has a number of questions to ask you, and do not try to take up all the interview time by showing off your extensive knowledge of the answer to the first one.

7) Be attentive

You only have 20 minutes or so, and you should keep your attention at its sharpest throughout. When a member is addressing a problem or question to you, give him your undivided attention. Address your reply principally to him, but do not exclude the other board members.

8) Do not interrupt

A board member may be stating a problem for you to analyze. He will ask you a question when the time comes. Let him state the problem, and wait for the question.

9) Make sure you understand the question

Do not try to answer until you are sure what the question is. If it is not clear, restate it in your own words or ask the board member to clarify it for you. However, do not haggle about minor elements.

10) Reply promptly but not hastily

A common entry on oral board rating sheets is "candidate responded readily," or "candidate hesitated in replies." Respond as promptly and quickly as you can, but do not jump to a hasty, ill-considered answer.

11) Do not be peremptory in your answers

A brief answer is proper – but do not fire your answer back. That is a losing game from your point of view. The board member can probably ask questions much faster than you can answer them.

12) Do not try to create the answer you think the board member wants

He is interested in what kind of mind you have and how it works – not in playing games. Furthermore, he can usually spot this practice and will actually grade you down on it.

13) Do not switch sides in your reply merely to agree with a board member

Frequently, a member will take a contrary position merely to draw you out and to see if you are willing and able to defend your point of view. Do not start a debate, yet do not surrender a good position. If a position is worth taking, it is worth defending.

14) Do not be afraid to admit an error in judgment if you are shown to be wrong

The board knows that you are forced to reply without any opportunity for careful consideration. Your answer may be demonstrably wrong. If so, admit it and get on with the interview.

15) Do not dwell at length on your present job

The opening question may relate to your present assignment. Answer the question but do not go into an extended discussion. You are being examined for a *new* job, not your present one. As a matter of fact, try to phrase ALL your answers in terms of the job for which you are being examined.

Basis of Rating

Probably you will forget most of these "do's" and "don'ts" when you walk into the oral interview room. Even remembering them all will not ensure you a passing grade. Perhaps you did not have the qualifications in the first place. But remembering them will help you to put your best foot forward, without treading on the toes of the board members.

Rumor and popular opinion to the contrary notwithstanding, an oral board wants you to make the best appearance possible. They know you are under pressure – but they also want to see how you respond to it as a guide to what your reaction would be under the pressures of the job you seek. They will be influenced by the degree of poise you display, the personal traits you show and the manner in which you respond.

ABOUT THIS BOOK

This book contains tests divided into Examination Sections. Go through each test, answering every question in the margin. At the end of each test look at the answer key and check your answers. On the ones you got wrong, look at the right answer choice and learn. Do not fill in the answers first. Do not memorize the questions and answers, but understand the answer and principles involved. On your test, the questions will likely be different from the samples. Questions are changed and new ones added. If you understand these past questions you should have success with any changes that arise. Tests may consist of several types of questions. We have additional books on each subject should more study be advisable or necessary for you. Finally, the more you study, the better prepared you will be. This book is intended to be the last thing you study before you walk into the examination room. Prior study of relevant texts is also recommended. NLC publishes some of these in our Fundamental Series. Knowledge and good sense are important factors in passing your exam. Good luck also helps. So now study this Passbook, absorb the material contained within and take that knowledge into the examination. Then do your best to pass that exam.

_____

EXAMINATION SECTION

EXAMINATION SECTION
TEST 1

DIRECTIONS: Each question or incomplete statement is followed by several suggested answers or completions. Select the one that BEST answers the question or completes the statement. *PRINT THE LETTER OF THE CORRECT ANSWER IN THE SPACE AT THE RIGHT.*

1. With a management staff of 15 capable analysts, which of the following organizational approaches would generally be BEST for overall results?
Organization

    A. by specialists in fields, such as management, organization, systems analysis
    B. by clientele to be served, such as hospitals, police, education, social services
    C. where all 15 report directly to head of the management staff
    D. by specialized study groups with flexibility in assigning staff under a qualified project leader

1.____

2. In conducting a general management survey to identify problems and opportunities, which of the following would it be LEAST necessary to consider?

    A. Identifying program and planning deficiencies in each functional area
    B. Organization problems
    C. Sound management practices not being used
    D. The qualifications of the supervisory personnel

2.____

3. Which of the following statements MOST accurately defines *operations research?*

    A. A highly sophisticated system used in the analysis of management problems
    B. A specialized application of electronic data processing in the analysis of management problems
    C. Research on operating problems
    D. The application of sophisticated mathematical tools to the analysis of management problems

3.____

4. Theoretically, an ideal organization structure can be set up for each enterprise. In actual practice, the ideal organization structure is seldom, if ever, obtained. Of the following, the one that is of LEAST influence in determining the organization structure is the

    A. existence of agreements and favors among members of the organization
    B. funds available
    C. growing trend of management to discard established forms in favor of new forms
    D. opinions and beliefs of top executives

4.____

5. To which one of the following is it MOST important that the functional or technical staff specialist in a large organization devote major attention?

    A. Conducting audits of line operations
    B. Controlling of people in the line organization
    C. Developing improved approaches, plans, and procedures and assisting the line organization in their implementation
    D. Providing advice to his superior and to operating units

5.____

6. In the planning for reorganization of a department, which one of the following principles relating to the assignment of functions is NOT correct?

    A. Line and staff functions should be separated.
    B. Separate functions should be assigned to separate organizational units.
    C. There should be no disturbance of the previously assigned tasks of personnel.
    D. There should generally be no overlapping among organizational elements.

6._____

7. Results are BEST accomplished within an organization when the budgets and plans are developed by the

    A. budget office, independent of the operating units
    B. head of the operating unit based on analysis of prior year's operations after discussion with his superior
    C. head of the operating unit with general guidelines and data from higher authority and the budget office, and input from key personnel
    D. head of the organization unit based on an analysis of prior year's operations

7._____

8. The *management process* is a term used to describe the responsibilities common to

    A. all levels of management
    B. first line supervisors
    C. middle management jobs
    D. top management jobs

8._____

9. Of the following, committees are BEST used for

    A. advising the head of the organization
    B. improving functional work
    C. making executive decisions
    D. making specific planning decisions

9._____

10. Which of the following would NOT be a part of a management control system?

    A. An objective test of new ideas or methods in operation
    B. Determination of need for organization improvement
    C. Objective comparison of operating results
    D. Provision of information useful for revising objectives, programs, and operations

10._____

11. Of the following, the one which a line role generally does NOT include is

    A. controlling results and performance
    B. coordinating work and exchanging ideas with other line organizations
    C. implementation of approved plans developed by staff
    D. planning work and making operating decisions

11._____

12. In a normal curve, one standard deviation would include MOST NEARLY what percentage of the cases Involved?

    A. 50%   B. 68%   C. 95%   D. 99%

12._____

13. The Office Layout Chart is a sketch of the physical arrangements of the office to which has been added the flow lines of the principal work performed there.
Which one of the following states the BEST advantage of superimposing the work flow onto the desk layout?

13._____

A. Lighting and acoustics can be improved.
B. Line and staff relationships can be determined.
C. Obvious misarrangements can be corrected.
D. The number of delays can be determined,

14. An advantage of the Multiple Process Chart over the Flow Process Chart is that the Multiple Process Chart shows the   14.____

A. individual worker's activity
B. number of delays
C. sequence of operations
D. simultaneous flow of work in several departments

15. Of the following, which is the MAJOR advantage of a microfilm record retention system?   15.____

A. Filing can follow the terminal digit system.
B. Retrieving documents from the files is faster.
C. Significant space is saved in storing records.
D. To read a microfilm record, a film reader is not necessary.

16. Which one of the following questions should the management analyst generally consider FIRST?   16.____

A. How is it being done? and Why should it be done that way?
B. What is being done? and Why is it necessary?
C. When should this job be done? and Why?
D. Who should do the job? and Why should he do it?

17. Assume that you are in the process of eliminating unnecessary forms.   17.____
The answer to which one of the following questions would be LEAST relevant?

A. Could the information be obtained elsewhere?
B. Is the form properly designed?
C. Is the form used as intended?
D. Is the purpose of the form essential to the operation?

18. Use of color in forms adds to their cost. Sometimes, however, the use of color will greatly   18.____
simplify procedure and more than pay for itself in time saved and errors eliminated.
This is ESPECIALLY true when

A. a form passes through many reviewers
B. considerable sorting is required
C. the form is other than a standard size
D. the form will not be sent through the mail

19. Of the following techniques, the one GENERALLY employed and considered BEST in   19.____
forms design is to divide writing lines into boxes with captions printed in small type
_____ of the box,

A. centered in the lower part
B. centered in the upper part
C. in the upper lefthand corner
D. in the lower righthand corner

3

20. Many forms authorities advocate the construction of a functional forms file or index. If such a file is set up, the MOST effective way of classifying forms for such an index is classification by   20.____

    A. department
    B. form number
    C. name or type of form
    D. subject to which the form applies

21. An interrelated pattern of jobs which makes up the structure of a system is known as   21.____

    A. a chain of command
    B. cybernetics
    C. the formal organization
    D. the maintenance pattern

22. A transparent sheet of film containing multiple rows of microimages is characteristic of which one of the following types of microfilm?   22.____

    A. Aperture   B. Jacket
    C. Microfiche   D. Roll or reel

23. PRIMARY responsibility for training and development of employees generally rests with   23.____

    A. outside training agencies
    B. the individual who needs training
    C. the line supervisor
    D. the training specialist in the Personnel Office

24. Which of the following approaches usually provides the BEST communication in the objectives and values of a new program which is to be introduced?   24.____

    A. A general written description of the program by the program manager for review by those who share responsibility
    B. An effective verbal presentation by the program manager to those affected
    C. Development of the plan and operational approach in carrying out the program by the program manager assisted by his key subordinates
    D. Development of the plan by the program manager's supervisor

25. The term *total systems concept,* as used in electronic data processing, refers   25.____

    A. only to the computer and its associated electronic accessories
    B. only to the paper information output, or *software* aspect
    C. to a large computer-based information handling system, which supplies the information needs of an entire agency or corporation
    D. to all of the automated and manual information systems in a specific sub-division of an organization

26. Of the following, scientific management can BEST be considered as an attempt to establish work procedures   26.____

    A. in fields of scientific endeavors
    B. which are beneficial only to bosses
    C. which require less control
    D. utilizing the concept of a man-machine system

27. The MAJOR failing of efficiency engineering was that it 　　　27.____

    A. overlooked the human factor
    B. required experts to implement the techniques
    C. was not based on true scientific principles
    D. was too costly and time consuming

28. Which of the following organizations is MOST noted throughout the world for its training 　28.____
in management?

    A. American Management Association
    B. American Political Science Association
    C. Society for the Advancement of Management
    D. Systems and Procedures Association

29. The GENERAL method of arriving at program objectives should be 　　29.____

    A. a trial and error process
    B. developed as the program progresses
    C. included in the program plan
    D. left to the discretion of the immediate supervisors

30. The review and appraisal of an organization to determine waste and deficiencies, 　30.____
improved methods, better means of control, more efficient operations, and greater use of
human and physical facilities is known as a(n)

    A. management audit
    B. manpower survey
    C. work simplification study
    D. operations audit

31. When data are grouped into a frequency distribution, the *median* is BEST defined as the 　31.____
_____ in the distribution.

    A. 50% point
    B. largest single range
    C. smallest single range
    D. point of greatest concentration

32. The manual, visual, and mental elements into which an operation may be analyzed in 　32.____
time and motion study are denoted by the term

    A. measurement   B. positioning
    C. standards   D. therbligs

33. Of the following, the symbol shown at the right, as used in a sys- 　　33.____
tems flow chart, denotes
    A. decision
    B. document
    C. manual operation
    D. process

34. Of the following agencies of city government, the one with the LARGEST expense budget for the current fiscal year is the   34.____

    A. environmental protection administration
    B. department of social services
    C. municipal service administration   previous
    D. police department

35. A feasibility study is the first phase in the process of conversion from manual to computerized data processing.   35.____
    The phases, in sequence, are the feasibility study,

    A. system conversion, system installation, follow up
    B. system design, installation
    C. system design, follow up, installation
    D. system design, system conversion, installation

36.   36.____

NAME OF WORKER	1st Hour	2nd Hour	3rd Hour	4th Hour	5th Hour	6th Hour	7th Hour	8th Hour
J. Jones								
B. Brown								
R. Roe								

The type of chart illustrated above is generally known as a _____ Chart.

    A. Flow   B. Gantt
    C. Work Simplification   D. Motion-Time Study

37.   37.____

ACTIVITY OF WORKER	TIME SCALE	ACTIVITY OF MACHINE WOOD LATHE
SELECT WOOD 1X1X9	.3	IDLE
SET WOOD BETWEEN CENTERS	.6	
START LATHE		TURNING FOR TEST CUT
ADJUST CENTERS	.9	IDLE
	1.2	
	1.5	
HOLD CUTTING TOOL ON REST		TURNING
	1.8	
	2.1	
STOP LATHE. TAKE LEG FROM LATHE AND PUT IN BOX	2.4	IDLE
	2.7	

MINUTES

The type of chart illustrated on the previous page is generally known as a _____ Chart.

    A. Flow   B. Gantt
    C. Simo   D. Work Simplification

38.   38.____

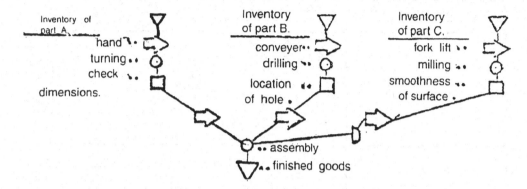

The type of chart illustrated above is generally known as a(n) _____ Chart.

    A. Multiple Activity   B. Motion-Time
    C. Work Place Layout   D. Operation Process

39.   39.____

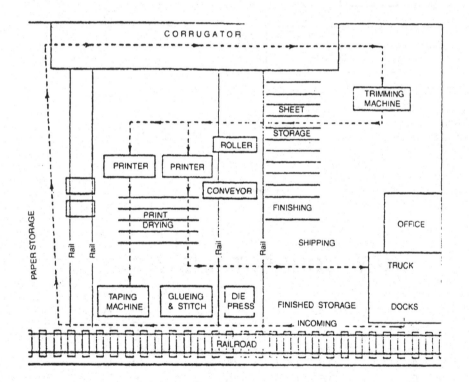

The one illustrated above is generally known as a

    A. Gantt Chart   B. Multiple Activity Chart
    C. Planned Flow Diagram   D. Work Place Diagram

40.   40.____

	PRESENT		PROPOSED		DIFFERENCE	
	NO.	Time	No.	Time	No.	Time
OPERATIONS						
TRANSPORTATIONS						
INSPECTIONS						
DELAYS						
STORAGES						
DISTANCE TRAVELLED		Ft.		Ft.		Ft.

JOB

CHART BEGINS
CHART ENDS
CHARTED BY
DATE

DETAILS OF {PRESENT / PROPOSED} METHOD	OPERATION TRANSPORT INSPECTION DELAY STORAGE	DISTANCE BY FEET	TIME BY MINUTES	DETAILS OF {PRESENT / PROPOSED} METHOD	OPERATION TRANSPORT INSPECTION DELAY STORAGE	DISTANCE BY FEET	TIME BY MINUTES
1.	O ⇨ ☐ D ▽		1.		O ⇨ ☐ D ▽	
2.	O ⇨ ☐ D ▽		2.		O ⇨ ☐ D ▽	
3.	O ⇨ ☐ D ▽		3.		O ⇨ ☐ D ▽	
4.	O ⇨ ☐ D ▽		4.		O ⇨ ☐ D ▽	
5.	O ⇨ ☐ D ▽		5.		O ⇨ ☐ D ▽	
6.	O ⇨ ☐ D ▽		6.		O ⇨ ☐ D ▽	
7.	O ⇨ ☐ D ▽		7.		O ⇨ ☐ D ▽	
8.	O ⇨ ☐ D ▽		8.		O ⇨ ☐ D ▽	

The type of chart illustrated above is generally known as a(n) _____ Chart.

A.   Analysis   B.   Flow Process
C.   Man or Material   D.   Multiple Activity

KEY (CORRECT ANSWERS)

1.	D	11.	B	21.	C	31.	A
2.	D	12.	B	22.	C	32.	D
3.	D	13.	C	23.	C	33.	A
4.	C	14.	D	24.	C	34.	B
5.	C	15.	C	25.	C	35.	D
6.	C	16.	B	26.	D	36.	B
7.	C	17.	B	27.	A	37.	C
8.	A	18.	B	28.	A	38.	D
9.	A	19.	C	29.	C	39.	C
10.	B	20.	D	30.	A	40.	B

TEST 2

DIRECTIONS: Each question or incomplete statement is followed by several suggested answers or completions. Select the one that BEST answers the question or completes the statement. *PRINT THE LETTER OF THE CORRECT ANSWER IN THE SPACE AT THE RIGHT.*

1. The one of the following which is MOST important in getting a systems survey off to a good start is

   A. a kick-off meeting with key personnel covering the purpose of the study and introduction of the survey staff
   B. a prior knowledge of the organization manual, charts, and statements of responsibility
   C. knowledge of personality problems in the agency needing special attention
   D. written announcement from the agency head

1.____

2. Which of the following is the LEAST important factor in planning an administrative survey?

   A. Developing a work plan and time schedule
   B. Knowledge of sound organization concepts and principles
   C. Survey techniques and methods to be used for analysis in compiling data needed
   D. The purpose, scope, and level of the survey

2.____

3. Assume that a supervisor, when reviewing a decision reached by one of his subordinates, finds the decision incorrect.
   Under these circumstances, it would be MOST desirable for the supervisor to

   A. correct the decision and inform the subordinate of this at a staff meeting
   B. correct the decision and suggest a more detailed analysis in the future
   C. help the employee find the reason for the correct decision
   D. refrain from assigning this type of problem to the employee

3.____

4. After an analyst has identified a problem area, which one of the following is the MOST important step in getting management to recognize that a problem does exist?

   A. A brief statement describing the problem
   B. Implications if problem is not corrected
   C. Relationship to other problems
   D. Supporting factual evidence and data indicating that the problem does exist

4.____

5. The statement, *work expands to fit the time available for its completion*, refers MOST directly to

   A. job enlargement principles
   B. Parkinson's Law
   C. The Open System Theory
   D. The Peter Principle

5.____

6. A comprehensive and constructive examination of a company, institution, or branch of government, or of any of its components such as an agency, division, or department, and its plans and objectives, methods of control, its means of operations, and its use of human and physical facilities is COMMONLY known as a(n) _____ audit.

    A. systems
    B. extensive financial
    C. operational or management
    D. organizational

6.____

7. Assume you are assigned to analyze the details of the procedures a clerk follows in order to complete filling out an invoice or a requisition. Your purpose is to simplify and shorten the procedure he has been trained to use.
The MOST appropriate chart for this purpose would be the

    A. block flow diagram
    C. forms flow chart
    B. flow process chart
    D. work distribution chart

7.____

8. In identifying problems and opportunities for improvement, which one of the following is MOST closely related to organization planning?

    A. Effective operating procedures issued from headquarters
    B. Effective records management
    C. Need for improved management concepts and practices
    D. Review of the salary and wage administration program

8.____

9. MOST of the working time of the functional or technical staff specialist in a large organization should be focused on

    A. conducting audits of line operations
    B. developing improved approaches, plans, and procedures and assisting the line organization in their implementation
    C. providing advice to his superior and to operating units
    D. the number of people in the line organization

9.____

10. The LEAST effective way for a survey group to plan is to

    A. clarify objectives and identify problems
    B. conduct planning and review sessions annually when budgets are prepared
    C. periodically conduct review sessions for purposes of coordination
    D. undertake specific action programs

10.____

11. Which one of the following is the MOST important element of a good manpower plan?

    A. Establishing inventories of capable personnel
    B. Forecasting the number of people needed in the future
    C. Having the right people for all jobs when needed
    D. Identifying training needs

11.____

12. Completed staff work is MOST effective in accomplishing which one of the following?

    A. Determination of the problems of the line organization
    B. Determination of the staffing needs of an organization
    C. Preparation of effective proposals and approaches to improve line results
    D. Review of budgets proposed by line organization

12.____

13. What generally is the PRINCIPAL objection to the use of form letters?   13._____
    The

    A. difficulty of developing a form letter to serve the purpose
    B. excessive time involved in selecting the proper form letter
    C. errors in selecting form letters
    D. impersonality of form letters

14. What is the BEST approach for introducing change?   14._____
    A

    A. combination of written and also verbal communication to all personnel affected by
       the change
    B. general bulletin to all personnel
    C. meeting pointing out all the values of the new approach
    D. written directive to key personnel

15. The FIRST step in designing an effective management survey is   15._____

    A. examining backlogs
    B. flow charting
    C. motion analysis and time study
    D. project planning

16. In statistical sampling, the error which will NOT be exceeded by 50 percent of the cases   16._____
    is known as the

    A. difference between two means
    B. probable error
    C. standard deviation
    D. standard error of the mean

17. In a normal or bell-shaped curve, the area encompassed by two standard deviations   17._____
    from the mean is

    A. 68%   B. 95%   C. 97%   D. 99%

18. The statistical average referring to that point on the scale at which the concentration is   18._____
    greatest or that value which occurs the greatest number of times and which might be
    taken as typical of the entire distribution is called the

    A. mean   B. median   C. mode   D. quartile

19. In process charting, the symbol which is used when con-ditions (except those which   19._____
    intentionally change the physical or chemical characteristics of the object) do not permit
    or require immediate performance is

    A.   B.   C.   D.

20. Assume that you are making a study of a central headquarters office which processes claims received from a number of district offices. You notice the following problems: Some employees are usually busy, while others doing the same kind of work in the same grade have little to do, high level professional people frequently spend considerable time searching for files in the file room. Which of the following charts would be MOST useful to record and analyze the data needed to help solve these problems? _____ Chart.

    A. Forms Distribution   B. Process
    C. Space Layout   D. Work Distribution

20.____

21. Which of the following types of work would NOT be readily measured by conventional time study techniques?
Work

    A. of sufficient volume, uniform in nature, that will justify the cost of continuing and maintaining controls
    B. that is countable in precise quantitative terms
    C. that is essentially creative and considerably varied in content
    D. that is repetitive, uniform, and homogeneous in content over a period of time

21.____

22. Which of the following should be the FIRST consideration in a work simplification study?
Can the

    A. sequence be changed for improvement?
    B. task be combined with another?
    C. task be eliminated?
    D. task be simplified?

22.____

23. In evaluating the sequence of operations involved in the clerical processing, which of the items listed below would be an indicator that methods improvements are needed?

    A. Some operations duplicate previous operations.
    B. The supervisor believes many of the company's policies are wrong.
    C. There is a high turnover of mail clerks.
    D. Work is logged into and out of the department.

23.____

24. Of the following, the one that is MOST likely to make a methods change unacceptable is when the

    A. change does not threaten the workers' security
    B. change follows a series of previously unsuccessful similar changes
    C. change has been well thought out and properly introduced
    D. people affected by the change have participated in the development of the changes

24.____

25. Which of the following questions has the LEAST significant bearing on the analysis of the paperwork flow?

    A. How is the work brought into the department and how is it taken away?
    B. How many work stations are involved in processing the work within the department?
    C. Is the work received and removed in the proper quantity?
    D. Where is the supervisor's desk located in relationship to those he supervises?

25.____

26. Which of the following does NOT have significant bearing on the arrangement, sequence, and zoning of information into box captions?
The

    A. layout of the source documents from which the infor-mation is taken
    B. logical flow of data
    C. needs of forms to be prepared from this form
    D. type of print to be employed

26.____

27. In determining the spacing requirements of a form and the size of the boxes to be used, PRIMARY consideration should be given to the

    A. distribution of the form
    B. method of entry, i.e., handwritten or machine and type of machine
    C. number of copies
    D. number of items to be entered

27.____

28. Of the following, the BEST technique to follow when providing instructions for the completion and routing of a form is to _____ the form.

    A. imprint the instructions on the face of
    B. imprint the instructions on the back of
    C. provide a written procedure to accompany
    D. provide verbal instructions when issuing

28.____

29. A forms layout style where a separate space in the shape of a box is provided for each item of information requested and the caption or question for each item is shown in the upper lefthand corner of each box is known as the _____ style.

    A. box   B. checkbox
    C. checklist   D. checkbox and checklist

29.____

30. It is the office manager's responsibility to promote office safety and eliminate hazards. A number of policies and procedures are widely advocated and followed by management and safety experts.
Of the following, the policy or procedure that is LEAST valid is:

    A. Each department supervisor should be required to complete a report at the time of each accident so that the person in charge of safety administration will be able to analyze the pattern of common causes and improve safety conditions
    B. Electrical cords and connectors for machines and equipment should be routinely checked so as to eliminate fire and shock hazards
    C. Employees should be informed of the type of acci-dents which may occur
    D. Smoking at desks should be prohibited so as to avoid the possibility of fire hazards; and a lounge provided for this purpose

30.____

31. An effective discussion leader is one who

    A. announces the problem and his preconceived solution at the start of the discussion
    B. guides and directs the discussion according to pre-arranged outline
    C. interrupts or corrects confused participants to save time
    D. permits anyone to say anything at anytime

31.____

32. Under what circumstances would it be MOST advisable to have two or more clerks in a department share the same adding machine?
When

    A. capital appropriations are tight
    B. the clerks sharing the adding machine are located at adjacent desks
    C. the clerks sharing the adding machine get along with one another
    D. the need for the equipment is so little that there is negligible time lost in sharing the adding machine

32.____

33. Of the following, the statement that is MOST descriptive of, and fundamental to, proper office landscaping is:

    A. All clerical desks should be arranged singly and in rows
    B. The layout should be built around the flow of infor-mation and work in the office
    C. The layout should be built around the recognized organizational hierarchy of the office unit
    D. There should be many planters arranged to give the office an open look

33.____

34. The MOST significant factor to be considered in deciding on an electric typewriter is the

    A. ability of some electric typewriters to change type face
    B. prestige typists associate with an electric type-writer
    C. standardization of type face
    D. volume of work to be performed by the typist

34.____

35. The human relations movement in management theory is BASICALLY concerned with

    A. counteracting employee unrest
    B. eliminating the *time and motion* man
    C. interrelationships among individuals in organizations
    D. the psychology of the worker

35.____

36. PERT, as commonly used, stood for

    A. Periodic Estimate of Resource Trends
    B. Potential Energy Research Technology
    C. Professional Engineer Review Tests
    D. Program Evaluation and Review Technique

36.____

37. The BEST type of chart to use in showing the absolute movement or change of a continuous series of data over a period of time, such as changes in prices, employment or expenses, is usually a _____ chart.

    A. bar   B. line
    C. multiple bar   D. pie

37.____

38. A computer language that was ESPECIALLY designed for third generation computers to enable their capabilities to be effectively utilized is

    A. BASIC   B. COBOL   C. FORTRAN   D. PL/1

38.____

39. An analog computer computes by making measurements on   39.____

    A. a storage drum
    B. magnetic tape
    C. punched cards
    D. some parallel physical system

40. The ONLY basic arithmetic operations performed by digital computers are   40.____

    A. addition and subtraction
    B. addition, subtraction, multiplication, and division
    C. exponential equations
    D. multiplication and division

KEY (CORRECT ANSWERS)

1.	A	11.	C	21.	C	31.	B
2.	B	12.	C	22.	C	32.	D
3.	C	13.	D	23.	A	33.	B
4.	D	14.	A	24.	B	34.	D
5.	B	15.	D	25.	D	35.	C
6.	C	16.	B	26.	D	36.	D
7.	B	17.	B	27.	B	37.	B
8.	C	18.	C	28.	A	38.	D
9.	B	19.	C	29.	A	39.	D
10.	B	20.	D	30.	D	40.	A

EXAMINATION SECTION
TEST 1

DIRECTIONS: Each question or incomplete statement is followed by several suggested answers or completions. Select the one that BEST answers the question or completes the statement. *PRINT THE LETTER OF THE CORRECT ANSWER IN THE SPACE AT THE RIGHT.*

1. In performing a systems study, the analyst may find it necessary to prepare an accurate record of working statistics from departmental forms, questionnaires, and information gleaned in interviews.
Which one of the following statements dealing with the statistical part of the study is the MOST valid?

    A. The emphasis of every survey is data collection.
    B. Data should not be represented in narrative form.
    C. The statistical report should include the titles of personnel required for each processing task.
    D. In gathering facts, the objective of a systems study should be the primary consideration.

1.____

2. The most direct method of obtaining information about activities in the area under study is by observation. There are several general rules for an analyst that are essential for observing and being accepted as an observer.
The one of the following statements relating to this aspect of an analyst's responsibility that is most valid in the initial phase is that the analyst should NOT

    A. limit himself to observing only; he may criticize operations and methods
    B. prepare himself for what he is about to observe
    C. obtain permission of the department's management to actually perform some of the clerical tasks himself
    D. offer views of impending charges regarding new staff requirements, equipment, or procedures

2.____

3. The active concern of the systems analyst is the study and documentation of what he observes as it exists. Before attempting the actual study and documentation, the analyst should comply with certain generally accepted procedures.
Of the following, the step the analyst should *generally* take FIRST is to

    A. define the problem and prepare a statement of objectives
    B. confer with the project director concerning persons to be interviewed
    C. accumulate data from all available sources within the area under study
    D. meet with operations managers to enlist their cooperation

3.____

4. During the course of any systems study, the analyst will have to gather some statistics if the operation model is to be realistic and meaningful.
With respect to the statistical report part of the study, it is MOST valid to say that

    A. it must follow a standard format since there should be no variation from one study to the next
    B. the primary factor to be considered is the volume of work in the departmental unit at each stage of completion
    C. only variations that occur during peak and slow periods should be recorded
    D. unless deadlines in the departmental units studied by the analyst occur constantly, they should not be taken into account

4.____

5. In systems analysis, the interview is one of the analyst's major sources of information. In conducting an interview, he should strive for immediate rapport with the operations manager or department head with whom he deals.
With respect to his responsibility in this area, it is considered LEAST appropriate for the analyst to

    5._____

    A. explain the full background of the study and the scope of the investigation
    B. emphasize the importance of achieving the stated objectives and review the plan of the project
    C. assume that the attitudes of the workers are less important than those of the executives
    D. request the manager's assistance in the form of questions, suggestions, and general cooperation

6. Large, complex endeavors often take a long time to implement. The following statements relate to long lead times imposed by large-scale endeavors.
Select the one usually considered to be LEAST valid.

    6._____

    A. Where there are external sponsors who provide funds or political support, they should be provided with some demonstration of what is being accomplished.
    B. Long lead times simplify planning and diminish the threat of obsolescence by assuring that objectives will be updated by the time the project is nearing completion.
    C. During the period when no tangible results are forthcoming, techniques must be found to assess progress.
    D. Employees, particularly scientific personnel, should feel a sense of accomplishment or they may shy away from research which involves long-term commitments.

7. In traditional management theory, administrators are expected to collect and weigh facts and probabilities, make an optimal decision and see that it is carried out.
In the management of large-scale development projects, such a clear sequence of action is *generally* NOT possible because of

    7._____

    A. their limited duration
    B. the static and fixed balance of power among interest groups
    C. continuous suppression of new facts
    D. constantly changing constraints and pressures

Questions 8–10.

DIRECTIONS: One of the most valuable parts of the systems package is the systems flowchart, a technique that aids understanding of the work flow. A flowchart should
depict all the intricacies of the work flow from start to finish in order to give the
onlooker a solid picture at a glance. The table below contains symbols used by
the analyst in flowcharting. In answering Questions 8 through 10, refer to the
following figures.

Figure I

Figure II

Figure III

Figure IV

Figure V

Figure VI

Figure VII

Figure VIII

Figure IX

Figure X

Figure XI

Figure XII

Figure XIII

8.   The symbol that is COMMONLY used to specify clerical procedures which are not essen-   8._____
tial to the main processing function and yet are part of the overall procedure is represented by Figure

   A.   III   B.   VI   C.   XII   D.   XIII

9.   An analyst wishes to designate the following activities: 9._____
File reports; Calculate average; Attach labels.
The MOST APPROPRIATE symbol to use is represented by Figure

   A.   V   B.   VI   C.   VII   D.   II

10.   A *Report, Journal,* or *Record* should be represented by Figure   10._____

   A.   I   B.   III   C.   IX   D.   XI

Question 11.

DIRECTIONS: The following figures are often used in program and systems flowcharting.

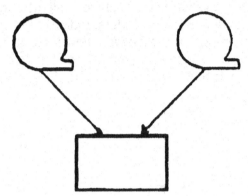

11.   The above figures represent   11._____

    A.   two magnetic tapes incorporated in a processing function
    B.   two report papers to be put in a cabinet in chronological order
    C.   two transmittal tapes—both externally generated—routed to a vault
    D.   an auxiliary operation involving two sequential decisions

12.   When research and analysis of government programs, e.g., pest control, drug rehabilita-   12._____
    tion, etc., is sponsored and conducted within a government unit, the scope of the analy-
    sis should *generally* be _____ the scope of the authority of the manager to whom the
    analyst is responsible.

    A.   less than   B.   less than or equal to
    C.   greater than or equal to   D.   greater than

13.   In recent years, there has been an increasing emphasis on outputs–the goods and ser-   13._____
    vices that a program produces. This emphasis on outputs imposes an information
    requirement. The one of the following which would MOST likely NOT be considered out-
    put information in a hospital or health care program is the

    A.   number of patients cared for
    B.   number of days patients were hospitalized
    C.   budgeted monies for hospital beds
    D.   quality of the service

14.   Which one of the following statements pertaining to management information systems is   14._____
    generally considered to be LEAST valid?

    A.   A management information system is a network of related subsystems developed
        according to an integrated scheme for evaluating the activities of an agency.
    B.   A management information system specifies the content and format, the prepara-
        tion and integration of information for all various functions within an agency that will
        best satisfy needs at various levels of management.
    C.   To operate a successful management information system, an agency will require a
        complex electronic computer installation.
    D.   The five elements which compose a management information system are: data
        input, files, data processing, procedures, and data output.

15. In the field of records management, electronic equipment is being used to handle office   15.____
paperwork or data processing. With respect to such use, of the following, it is MOST valid
to say that

    A. electronic equipment is not making great strides in the achievement of speed and
economy in office paperwork
    B. electronic equipment accelerates the rate at which office paperwork is completed
    C. paperwork problems can be completely solved through mechanization
    D. introduction of electronic data processing equipment cuts down on the paper con-
sumed in office processes

16. A reports control program evaluates the reporting requirements of top management so   16.____
that reviews can be made of the existing reporting system to determine its adequacy.
Of the following statements pertaining to reports control, which is the MOST likely to
be characteristic of such a program?

    A. Only the exception will be reported
    B. Preparation of daily reports will be promoted
    C. Executives will not delegate responsibility for preparing reports
    D. Normal conditions are reported

17. Which of the following types of work measurement techniques requires the HIGHEST   17.____
degree of training and skill of technicians and supervisors and is MOST likely to involve
the HIGHEST original cost?

    A. Work sampling
    B. Predetermined time standards
    C. The time study (stopwatch timing)
    D. Employee reporting

18. Which of the following types of work measurement techniques *generally* requires the   18.____
LEAST amount of time to measure and establish standards?

    A. Work sampling
    B. Predetermined time standards
    C. The time study (stopwatch timing)
    D. Employee reporting

19. Assume that you, as an analyst, have been assigned to formally organize small work   19.____
groups within a city department to perform a special project. After studying the project,
you find you must choose between two possible approaches–either task teams or highly
functionalized groups.
What would be one of the advantages of choosing the task-team approach over the
highly functionalized organization?

    A. Detailed, centralized planning would be encouraged.
    B. Indifference to city goals and restrictions on output would be lessened.
    C. Work would be divided into very specialized areas.
    D. Superiors would be primarily concerned with seeing that subordinates do not devi-
ate from the project.

20. In systems theory, there is a *what-if* method of treating uncertainty that explores the   20.____
effect on the alternatives of environmental change. This method is generally referred to
as _____ analysis.

    A. sensitivity   B. contingency
    C. a fortiori   D. systems

KEY (CORRECT ANSWERS)

1.	D		11.	A
2.	D		12.	B
3.	A		13.	C
4.	B		14.	C
5.	C		15.	B
6.	B		16.	A
7.	D		17.	B
8.	D		18.	A
9.	A		19.	B
10.	B		20.	B

TEST 2

DIRECTIONS: Each question or incomplete statement is followed by several suggested answers or completions. Select the one that BEST answers the question or completes the statement. *PRINT THE LETTER OF THE CORRECT ANSWER IN THE SPACE AT THE RIGHT.*

1. Which of the following systems exists at the strategic level of an organization?   1.____

   A. Decision support system (DSS)
   B. Executive support system (ESS)
   C. Knowledge work system (KWS)
   D. Management information system (MIS)

2. The functions of knowledge workers in an organization generally include each of the fol-   2.____
   lowing EXCEPT

   A. updating knowledge
   B. managing documentation of knowledge
   C. serving as internal consultants
   D. acting as change agents

3. Which of the following is not a management benefit associated with end-user develop-   3.____
   ment of information systems?

   A. Reduced application backlog
   B. Increased user satisfaction
   C. Simplified testing and documentation procedures
   D. Improved requirements determination

4. Assume that an analyst is preparing an analysis of a departmental program. His investi-   4.____
   gation leads him to a potential problem relating to the program. The analyst thinks the
   potential problem is so serious that he cannot rely on preventive actions to remove the
   cause or significantly reduce the probability of its occurrence.
   Of the following, the MOST appropriate way for the analyst to promptly handle this
   serious matter described above would be to

   A. apply systematic afterthought to the achievement of objectives by analysis of the
       problem
   B. compare actual performance with the expected standard of performance
   C. prepare contingency actions to be adopted immediately if the problem does occur
   D. identify, locate, and describe the deviation from the standard

5. Assume that an analyst is directed to investigate a problem relating to organizational   5.____
   behavior in his agency and to prepare a report thereon. After reviewing the preliminary
   draft, his superior cautions him to overcome his tendency to misuse and overgeneralize
   his interpretation of existing knowledge.
   Which one of the following statements appearing in the draft is MOST *usually* considered to be a common distortion of behavioral science knowledge?

   A. Pay—even incentive pay—isn't very important anymore.
   B. There are nonrational aspects to people's behavior.
   C. The informal system exerts much control over organizational participants.
   D. Employees have many motives.

Questions 6-10.

DIRECTIONS: Each of Questions 6 through 10 consists of a statement which contains one word that is incorrectly used because it is not in keeping with the meaning that the quotation is evidently intended to convey. Determine which word is incorrectly used. Then select from the words lettered A, B, C, or D the word which, when substituted for the incorrectly used word, would BEST help to convey the meaning of the statement.

6.   While the utilization of cost-benefit analysis in decision-making processes should be encouraged, it must be well understood that there are many limitations on the constraints of the analysis. One must be cautioned against using cost-benefit procedures automatically and blindly. Still, society will almost certainly be better off with the application of cost-benefit methods than it would be without them. As some authorities aptly point out, an important advantage of a cost-benefit study is that it forces those responsible to quantify costs and benefits as far as possible rather than rest content with vague qualitative judgments or personal hunches. Also, such an analysis has the very valuable by-product of causing questions to be asked which would otherwise not have been raised. Finally, even if cost-benefit analysis cannot give the right answer, it can sometimes play the purely negative role of screening projects and rejecting those answers which are obviously less promising.

6._____

   A.   precise   B.   externally
   C.   applicability   D.   unresponsiveness

7.   The programming method used by the government should attempt to assess the costs and benefits of individual projects, in comparison with private and other public alternatives. The program, then, consists of the most meritorious projects that the budget will design. Meritorious projects excluded from the budget provide arguments for increasing its size. There are difficulties inherent in the specific project approach. The attempt is to apply profit criteria in public projects analogous to those used in evaluating private projects. This involves comparison of monetary values of present and future costs and benefits. But, in many important cases, such as highways, parkways, and bridges, the product of the government's investment does not directly enter the market economy. Consequently, evaluation requires imputation of market values. For example, the returns on a bridge have been estimated by attempting to value the time saved by users. Such measurements necessarily contain a strong, element of artificiality.

7._____

   A.   annulled   B.   expedient   C.   accommodate   D.   marginally

8.   Consider the problem of budgeting for activities designed to alleviate poverty and rooted unemployment. Are skill retraining efforts better or worse investments than public works? Are they better or worse than subsidies or other special incentives to attract new industry? Or, at an even more fundamental level, is a dollar invested in an attempt to rehabilitate a mature, technologically displaced, educationally handicapped, unemployed man a better commitment than a comparable dollar invested in supporting the educational and technical preparation of his son for employment in a different line of work? The questions may look unreasonable, even unanswerable. But the fact is that they are implicitly answered in any budget decision in the defined problem area. The only subordinate issue is whether the answer rests on intuition and guess, or on a budget system that presents relevant information so organized as to contribute to rational analysis, planning, and decision-making.

8._____

   A.   incomplete   B.   relevant
   C.   significant   D.   speculate

9. Choices among health programs, on the basis of cost-benefit analysis, raise another set of ethical problems. Measuring discounted lifetime earnings does not reveal the value of alleviating pain and suffering; some diseases have a high death rate, others are debilitating, others are merely uncomfortable. In general, choices among health and education programs that are predicated on discounted lifetime earnings will structure the choice against those who have low earnings, those whose earnings will materialize only at some future point in time, or those whose participation in the labor force is limited. It may be an appropriate economic policy to reduce expenditures in areas that maximize the future level of national income. But the maximization of social welfare may dictate attention to considerations, such as equality of opportunity, that transcend the limitations of values defined in such narrow terms.

9._____

    A. concentrate   B. divergent   C. enforcing   D. favorably

10. Without defined and time-phased objectives, it is difficult to be critical of administrative performance. To level a charge of waste or malperformance at the managers of a public program is, of course, one of the more popular pastimes of any administration's loyal opposition. But it is a rare experience to find such a charge documented by the kind of precise cost-effectiveness measures that are the common test of the quality of management performance in a well-run organization. Those who take a professional view of management responsibility are even more concerned about the acceptance of the kind of information that would enable a manager to assess the progress and quality of his own performance and, as appropriate, to initiate corrective action before outside criticism can even start.

10._____

    A. absence   B. rebut   C. withdraw   D. impeded

11. What is the relationship between the cost of inputs and the value of outputs when the results obtained from a program can be measured in money? _____ ratio.

11._____

    A. Value administrative-cost   B. Break-even point
    C. Variable-direct   D. Cost-benefit

12. Some writers in the field of public expenditure have noted a disturbing tendency inherent in cost-benefit analysis. Which one of the following statements MOST accurately expresses their concern over the use of cost-benefit analysis? It

12._____

    A. encourages the attachment of monetary values to intangibles
    B. has a built-in neglect of measurable outcomes while emphasizing the nonmeasurable
    C. consciously exaggerates social values and overstates political values
    D. encourages emphasis of those costs and benefits that cannot be measured rather than those that can

13. In private industry, budgetary control begins logically with an estimate of sales and the income therefrom.
Of the following, the term used in government which is MOST analogous to that of sales in private industry is

13._____

    A. borrowed funds   B. the amount appropriated
    C. general overhead   D. surplus funds

14. When constructing graphs of causally related variables, how should the variables be placed to conform to conventional use?   14.___

    A. The independent variable should be placed on the vertical axis and the dependent variable on the horizontal axis.
    B. The dependent variable should be placed on the vertical axis and the independent variable on the horizontal axis.
    C. Independent variables should be placed on both axes.
    D. Dependent variables should be placed on both axes.

Questions 15–18.

DIRECTIONS: Answer Questions 15 through 18 on the basis of the following graph describing the output of computer operators.

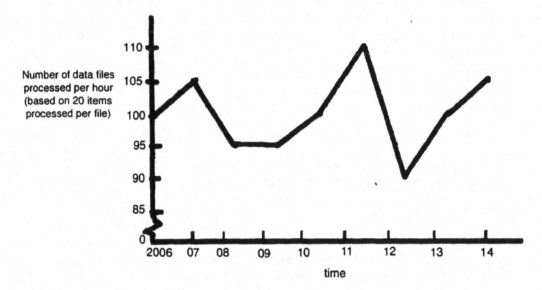

15. Of the following, during what four-year period did the AVERAGE OUTPUT of computer operators *fall below* 100 data files per hour?   15.___

    A. 2007-10   B. 2008-11   C. 2010-13   D. 2011-14

16. The AVERAGE PERCENTAGE CHANGE in output over the previous year's output for the years 2009 to 2012 is MOST NEARLY   16.___

    A. 2   B. 0   C. -5   D. -7

17. The DIFFERENCE between the actual output for 2012 and the projected figure based upon the average increase from 2006 to 2011 is MOST NEARLY   17.___

    A. 18   B. 20   C. 22   D. 24

18. Assume that after constructing the above graph, you, an analyst, discovered that the average number of items processed per file in 2012 was 25 (instead of 20) because of the complex nature of the work performed during that period.
The AVERAGE OUTPUT in files per hour for the period 2010 to 2013, expressed in terms of 20 items per file, would then be APPROXIMATELY   18.____

    A. 95   B. 100   C. 105   D. 110

19. Assume that Unit S's production fluctuated substantially from one year to another. In 2009, Unit S's production was 100% greater than in 2008; in 2010, it was 25% less than in 2009; and in 2011, it was 10% greater than in 2010. On the basis of this information, it is CORRECT to conclude that Unit S's production in 2011 exceeded its production in 2008 by   19.____

    A. 50%   B. 65%   C. 75%   D. 90%

20. Statistical sampling is often used in administrative operations primarily because it enables   20.____

    A. administrators to make staff selections
    B. decisions to be made based on mathematical and scientific fact
    C. courses of action to be determined by electronic data processing or computer pro-
        grams
    D. useful predictions to be made from relatively small samples

———————

KEY (CORRECT ANSWERS)

1.	B	11.	D
2.	B	12.	A
3.	C	13.	B
4.	C	14.	B
5.	A	15.	A
6.	C	16.	B
7.	C	17.	C
8.	C	18.	C
9.	A	19.	B
10.	A	20.	D

EXAMINATION SECTION
TEST 1

DIRECTIONS: Each question or incomplete statement is followed by several suggested answers or completions. Select the one that BEST answers the question or completes the statement. *PRINT THE LETTER OF THE CORRECT ANSWER IN THE SPACE AT THE RIGHT.*

1. Of the following, the BEST statement concerning the placement of *Conclusions and Recommendations* in a management report is:

   A. Recommendations should always be included in a report unless the report presents the results of an investigation
   B. If a report presents conclusions, it must present recommendations
   C. Every statement that is a conclusion should grow out of facts given elsewhere in the report
   D. Conclusions and recommendations should always conclude the report because they depend on its contents

   1.____

2. Assume you are preparing a systematic analysis of your agency's pest control program and its effect on eliminating rodent infestation of premises in a specific region.
   To omit from your report important facts which you originally received from the person to whom you are reporting is GENERALLY considered to be

   A. *desirable;* anyone who is likely to read the report can consult his files for extra information
   B. *undesirable;* the report should include major facts that are obtained as a result of your efforts
   C. *desirable;* the person you are reporting to does not
   D. pass the report on to others who lack his own familiarity with the subject
   E. *undesirable;* the report should include all of the facts that are obtained as a result of your efforts

   2.____

3. Of all the nonverbal devices used in report writing, tables are used most frequently to enable a reader to compare statistical information more easily. Hence, it is important that an analyst know when to use tables.
   Which one of the following statements that relate to tables is generally considered to be LEAST valid?

   A. A table from an outside source must be acknowledged by the report writer.
   B. A table should be placed far in advance of the point where it is referred to or discussed in the report.
   C. The notes applying to a table are placed at the bottom of the table, rather than at the bottom of the page on which the table is found.
   D. A table should indicate the major factors that effect the data it contains.

   3.____

4. Assume that an analyst writes reports which contain more detail than might be needed to serve their purpose.
   Such a practice is GENERALLY considered to be

   4.____

    A.   *desirable* ; this additional detail permits maximized machine utilization
    B.   *undesirable;* if specifications of reports are defined when they are first set up, loss of flexibility will follow
    C.   *desirable;* everything ought to be recorded so it will be there if it is ever needed
    D.   *undesirable;* recipients of these reports are likely to discredit them entirely

5.   Assume that an analyst is gathering certain types of information which can be obtained only through interrogation of the clientele by means of a questionnaire.
Which one of the following statements that relate to construction of the questionnaire is the MOST valid?   5._____

    A.   Stress, whenever possible, the use of leading questions.
    B.   Avoid questions which touch on personal prejudice or pride.
    C.   Opinions, as much as facts, should be sought.
    D.   There is no psychological advantage for starting with a question of high interest value.

Questions 6-10.

DIRECTIONS: Questions 6 through 10 consist of sentences lettered A, B, C, and D. For each question, choose the sentence which is stylistically and grammatically MOST appropriate for a management report.

6.   A.   For too long, the citizen has been forced to rely for his productivity information on the whims, impressions and uninformed opinion of public spokesmen.   6._____
    B.   For too long, the citizen has been forced to base his information about productivity on the whims, impressions and uninformed opinion of public spokesmen.
    C.   The citizen has been forced to base his information about productivity on the whims, impressions and uninformed opinion of public spokesmen for too long.
    D.   The citizen has been forced for too long to rely for his productivity information on the whims, impressions and uninformed opinion of public spokesmen.

7.   A.   More competition means lower costs to the city, thereby helping to compensate for inflation.   7._____
    B.   More competition, helping to compensate for inflation, means lower costs to the city.
    C.   Inflation may be compensated for by more competition, which will reduce the city's costs.
    D.   The costs to the city will be lessened by more competition, helping to compensate for inflation.

8.   A.   Some objectives depend on equal efforts from others, particularly private interests and the federal government; for example, technical advancement.   8._____
    B.   Some objectives, such as technical advancement, depend on equal efforts from others, particularly private interests and the federal government.
    C.   Some objectives depend on equal efforts from others, particularly private interests and the federal government, such as technical advancement.
    D.   Some objectives depend on equal efforts from others (technical advancement, for example); particularly private interests and the federal government.

9. A. It has always been the practice of this office toeffectuate recruitment of prospective employees from other departments.
    B. This office has always made a practice of recruiting prospective employees from other departments.
    C. Recruitment of prospective employees from other departments has always been a practice which has been implemented by this office.
    D. Implementation of the policy of recruitment of prospective employees from other departments has always been a practice of this office.

9._____

10. A. These employees are assigned to the level of work evidenced by their efforts and skills during the training period.
    B. The level of work to which these employees is assigned is decided upon on the basis of the efforts and skills evidenced by them during the period in which they were trained.
    C. Assignment of these employees is made on the basis of the level of work their efforts and skills during the training period has evidenced.
    D. These employees are assigned to a level of work their efforts and skills during the training period have evidenced.

10._____

11. To overcome the manual collation problem, forms are frequently padded.
    Of the following statements which relate to this type of packaging, select the one that is MOST accurate.

    A. Typewritten forms which are prepared as padded forms are more efficient than all other packaging.
    B. Padded forms are best suited for handwritten forms.
    C. It is difficult for a printer to pad form copies of different colors.
    D. Registration problems increase when cut-sheet forms are padded.

11._____

12. Most forms are cut from a standard mill sheet of paper.
    This is the size on which forms dealers base their prices. Since an agency is paying for a full-size sheet of paper, it is the responsibility of the analyst to design forms so that as many as possible may be cut from the sheet without waste.
    Of the following sizes, select the one that will cut from a standard mill sheet with the GREATEST waste and should, therefore, be avoided if possible.

    A. 4" x 6"   B. 5" x 8"   C. 9" x 12"   D. 8 1/2" x 14"

12._____

13. Assume that you are assigned the task of reducing the time and costs involved in completing a form that is frequently used in your agency. After analyzing the matter, you decide to reduce the writing requirements of the form through the use of ballot boxes and preprinted data.
    If exact copy-to-copy registration of this form is necessary, it is MOST advisable to

    A. vary the sizes of the ballot boxes
    B. stagger the ballot boxes
    C. place the ballot boxes as close together as possible
    D. have the ballot boxes follow the captions

13._____

31

14. To overcome problems that are involved in the use of cut-sheet and padded forms, spe-   14.____
cialty forms have been developed. Normally, these forms are commercially manufactured
rather than produced in-plant. Before designing a form as a specialty form, however, you
should be assured that certain factors are present.
Which one of the following factors deserves LEAST consideration?

   A. The form is to be used in quantities of 5,000 or more annually.
   B. The forms will be prepared on equipment using either a pinfeed device or pressure
      rollers for continuous feed-through.
   C. Two or more copies of the form set must be held together for further processing
      subsequent to the initial distribution of the form set.
   D. Copies of the form will be identical and no items of data will be selectively elimi-
      nated from one or more copies of the form.

15. Although a well-planned form should require little explanation as to its completion, there   15.____
are many occasions when the analyst will find it necessary to include instructions on the
form to assure that the person completing it does so correctly.
With respect to such instructions, it is usually considered to be LEAST appropriate to
place them

   A. in footnotes at the bottom of the form
   B. following the spaces to be completed
   C. directly under the form's title
   D. on the front of the form

16. One of the basic data-arrangement methods used in forms design is the *on-line* method.   16.____
When this method is used, captions appear on the same line as the space provided for
entry of the variable data.
This arrangement is NOT recommended because it

   A. forces the typist to make use of the typewriter's tab stops, thus increasing process-
      ing time
   B. wastes horizontal space since the caption appears on the writing line
   C. tends to make the variable data become more dominant than the captions
   D. increases the form's processing time by requiring the typist to continually roll the
      platen back and forth to expose the caption

17. Before designing a form for his agency, the analyst should be aware of certain basic   17.____
design standards.
Which one of the following statements relating to horizontal and vertical spacing
requirements is *generally* considered to be the MOST acceptable in forms design?

   A. If the form will be completed by typewriter, no more than four writing lines to the
      vertical inch should be allowed.
   B. If the form will be completed by hand, allowance should not be made for the differ-
      ent sizes of individual handwriting.
   C. If the form will be completed partly by hand and partly by typewriter, the analyst
      should provide the same vertical spacing as for typewriter completion
   D. The form should be designed with proportional spacing for pica and elite type.

18. As an analyst, you may be required to conduct a functional analysis of your agency's forms.
    Which one of the following statements pertaining to this type of analysis is *generally* considered to be MOST valid?

    A. Except for extremely low-volume forms, all forms should be functionally analyzed.
    B. To obtain maximum benefit from the analysis, functional re-analyses of all forms should be undertaken at least once every three to six months.
    C. All existing forms should be functionally analyzed before reorder.
    D. Only new forms should be functionally analyzed prior to being authorized for adoption.

18.____

19. The analyst must assure the users of a form that its construction provides for the most efficient method in terms of how data will be entered and processed subsequent to their initial entry.
    While the simplest construction is the cut sheet, the GREATEST disadvantage of this type of construction is

    A. the non-productive *makeready* time required if multiple copies of a form must be simultaneously prepared
    B. the difficulty experienced by users in filling in the forms solely by mechanical means
    C. its uneconomical cost of production
    D. the restrictions of limitations placed on the utilization of a variety of substances which may be used in form composition

19.____

20. Assume you have designed a form which requires data to be entered on multiple copies simultaneously. A determination has not yet been made whether to order the form as interleaved-carbon form sets or as carbonless forms.
    The advantage of using carbonless forms is that they

    A. permit more readable copies to be made at a single writing
    B. average about 30 percent lower in price than conventional interleaved-carbon form sets
    C. provide greater security if the information entered on the form is classified
    D. are not subject to accidental imaging

20.____

KEY (CORRECT ANSWERS)

1.	C		11.	B
2.	B		12.	C
3.	B		13.	B
4.	D		14.	D
5.	B		15.	A
6.	B		16.	B
7.	A		17.	C
8.	B		18.	C
9.	B		19.	A
10.	A		20.	C

———

TEST 2

DIRECTIONS: Each question or incomplete statement is followed by several suggested answers or completions. Select the one that BEST answers the question or completes the statement. *PRINT THE LETTER OF THE CORRECT ANSWER IN THE SPACE AT THE RIGHT.*

1. Many analysts lean toward the use of varying colors of paper in a multiple-part form set to indicate distribution. This usage is GENERALLY considered to be   1._____

   A. *desirable;* it is more effective than using white paper for all copies and imprinting the distribution in the margin of the copy
   B. *undesirable;* colored inks should be used instead to indicate distribution in a multi-part form set
   C. *desirable;* it will lead to lower costs of form production
   D. *undesirable;* it causes operational difficulties if the form is to be microfilmed or optically scanned

2. After a form has been reviewed and approved by the analyst, it should be given an identifying number. The following items pertain to the form number.   2._____
   Which item is MOST appropriately included as a portion of the form number?

   A. Revision date
   B. Order quantity
   C. Retention period
   D. Organization unit responsible for the form

Questions 3-8

DIRECTIONS: Questions 3 through 8 should be answered on the basis of the following information.

   Assume that the figure at the top of the next page is a systems flowchart specifically prepared for the purchasing department of a large municipal agency. Some of the symbols in the flowchart are incorrectly used. The symbols are numbered.

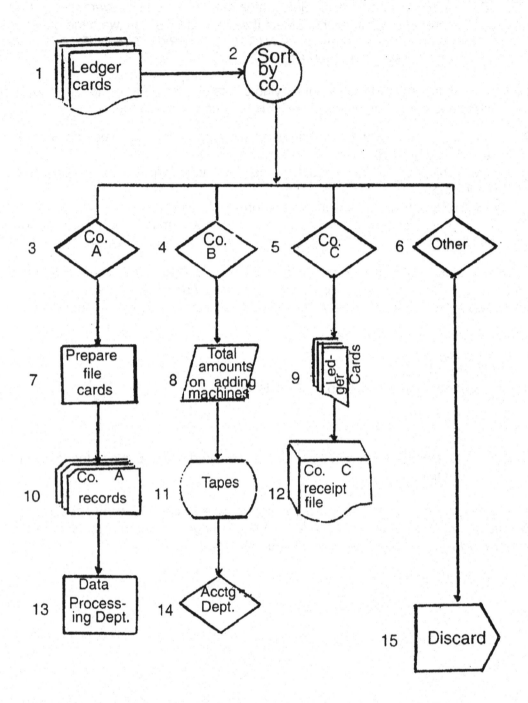

3. According to the flowchart, Number 2 is

    A. *correct*
    B. *incorrect;* the symbol should have six sides
    C. *incorrect;* the symbol should be the same as Number 7
    D. *incorrect;* the symbol should be the same as Number 8

3.____

4. According to the flowchart, Number 9 is

    A. *correct*
    B. *incorrect;* the symbol should be the same as Number 1

4.____

C. *incorrect;* the symbol should be the same as Number 7
D. *incorrect;* the symbol should be the same as Number 10

5. According to the flowchart, Number 11 is   5._____

    A. *correct*
    B. *incorrect;* the symbol should be the same as Number 13
    C. *incorrect;* the symbol should be the same as Number 10
    D. *incorrect;* the symbol should be the same as Number 9

6. According to the flowchart, Number 14 is   6._____

    A. *correct*
    B. *incorrect;* the symbol should have three sides
    C. *incorrect;* the symbol should have six sides
    D. *incorrect;* the symbol should have eight sides

7. According to the flowchart, Number 12 is   7._____

    A. *correct*
    B. *incorrect;* a *file* should be represented in the same form as the symbol which immediately precedes it
    C. *incorrect;* the symbol should be the same as Number 13
    D. *incorrect;* the symbol should be the same as Number 14

8. According to the flowchart, Number 15 is   8._____
    A. *correct*

    B. *incorrect;* the symbol should be

    C. *incorrect;* the symbol should be

    D. *incorrect;* the symbol should be

9. An agency expects to increase its services, the workload of the office will increase, and additional equipment and personnel will probably be required. Although there is no set formula for determining how much space will be required in an agency in a specific number of years from now, certain guidelines have been developed to assist the analyst in dealing with the problem of providing expansion space.
    Which of the following statements pertaining to this aspect of space utilization is *generally* considered to be the LEAST desirable practice?   9._____

    A. Spread the departments to fit into space that is temporarily surplus and awaiting the day when it is needed
    B. Place major departments where they can expand into the area of minor departments
    C. Visualize the direction in which the expansion will go and avoid placing the relatively fixed installations in the way
    D. Lay out the departments economically and screen off the surplus areas, using them for storage or other temporary usage

Questions 10-11.

DIRECTIONS: Questions 10 and 11 are based on the following layout.

Layout of Conference Room
BUREAU OF RODENT CONTROL

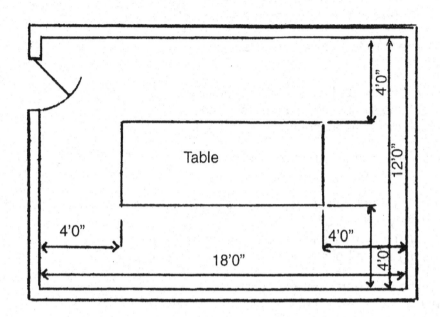

10. The LARGEST number of persons that can be accommodated in the area shown in the layout is

    A. 16   B. 10   C. 8   D. 6

10.____

11. Assume that the Bureau's programs undergo expansion and the Director indicates that the feasibility of increasing the size of the conference room should be explored.
For every two additional persons that are to be accommodated, the analyst should rec- ommend that _____ be added to table length and _____ be added to room length.

    A. 2'-6";2'-6"   B. 5'-0"; 5'-0"
    C. 2'-6"; 5'-0"   D. 5'-0"; 2'-6"

11.____

Questions 12-14.

DIRECTIONS: Questions 12 through 14 are based on the following information.

SYMBOLS USED IN LAYOUT WORK

Figure I ◯

Figure II ─◯

Figure III ⊙

Figure IV ▢

Figure V ─◯─

Figure VI ◁

Figure VII ⬚

Figure VIII

Figure IX ──────────

Figure X ─▨──▨──▨─

Figure XI ─▢──▢──▢─

Figure XII ⊠ ≡

12. Figure XI is the symbol for   12.____

    A. a temporary partition   B. floor outlets
    C. ceiling outlets   D. a switch

13. A *solid post* is represented by Figure   13.____

    A. II   B. V   C. VIII   D. XII

14. Figure VI is the symbol for a(n)   14.____

    A. switch   B. intercom
    C. telephone outlet   D. railing

15. While there is no one office layout that will fit all organizations, there are some reason-   15.____
ably good principles of office layout by function that could be applied to any office situation.
Which one of the following statements relating to functions and locations is MOST
characteristic of a good layout?
The

    A. personnel department is usually close to the reception area
    B. purchasing department should be far from the entrance
    C. data processing activity and duplicating services are normally placed together
    D. top management group is usually dispersed throughout the general office group

16. Records are valuable to an organization becaused recorded information is more accu-   16.____
rate and enduring than oral information.
Of the following, the MOST important stage in records management is at the

    A. storage stage
    B. time when quality control principles are applied
    C. point of distribution
    D. source when records are created

17. The rough layout of an office can be made by sketching the office floor plan from actual 17.____
measurements, or it can be copied from blueprints furnished by the building management.
As an analyst assigned to improve an office layout, you should be aware that the experienced layout man prefers to make his sketch from

    A. a blueprint because it eliminates the extra work in checking a sketch made from it
    B. actual measurements because a blueprint is in a scale of 1/4 or 1/2 inch to a foot
       instead of the preferred 1/8 inch scale
    C. a blueprint because he can always trust the blueprint
    D. actual measurements because he has to sketch in the desks and other equipment

18. Planning the traffic flow and appropriate aisle space in an office are factors an analyst 18.____
must consider in any desk arrangement.
Of the following, it is *generally* the MOST desirable practice to

    A. deny requests to rearrange desks to give employees more working space if the
       space left for the aisle is more than needed for the traffic
    B. figure operating space and the open file drawer separately from the allowance for
       the aisle if files must open into the aisle
    C. conserve space by making the main aisle in an office no wider than 36 inches
    D. disregard the length of feeders to an aisle in determining the width of the aisle

19. Code systems which are used to mark records for long- or short-term retention are easy 19.____
to devise and use.
Accordingly, of the following situations, it would be MOST appropriate to use the
destroy code for

    A. information that calls for action within 90 days and for which no record is necessary
       thereafter
    B. information that may be needed for evaluation of past agency activities
    C. records which contain information that is readily available elsewhere
    D. records that contain information necessary for audit requirements

20. Assume your agency is moving into new quarters and you will assist your superior in 20.____
assigning space to the various offices. The offices will be air-conditioned. The interior of
the space to be assigned is located away from windows.
Of the following, it is MOST appropriate for you to recommend that the interior of the
space be set aside for

    A. legal offices and confidential investigation sections
    B. visitors to the agency
    C. conference and training rooms
    D. typing and stenographic pools

KEY (CORRECT ANSWERS)

1.	D		11.	A
2.	A		12.	A
3.	A		13.	D
4.	B		14.	C
5.	D		15.	A
6.	C		16.	D
7.	A		17.	D
8.	C		18.	B
9.	A		19.	C
10.	B		20.	C

———

EXAMINATION SECTION
TEST 1

DIRECTIONS: Each question or incomplete statement is followed by several suggested answers or completions. Select the one that BEST answers the question or completes the statement. *PRINT THE LETTER OF THE CORRECT ANSWER IN THE SPACE AT THE RIGHT.*

1. An administrator in a department should be thoroughly familiar with modern methods of personnel administration. This statement is

    A. true, because this familiarity will help him in performing the normal functions of his office
    B. false, because personnel administration is not a departmental matter, but is centralized in the Civil Service Commission
    C. *true,* because this knowledge will insure the elimination of personnel problems in the department
    D. *false,* because departmental problems of a minor character are handled by the personnel representative, while major problems are the responsibility of the commissioner

1._____

2. The LEAST true of the following is that an administrative assistant in a department

    A. executes the policy laid down by the commissioner or his deputies
    B. in the main, carries out the policies of the commissioner but with some leeway where his own frame of reference is determinative
    C. is never required to formulate policy
    D. is responsible for the successful accomplishment of a section of the department's program

2._____

3. If a representative committee of employees in a large department is to meet with an administrative officer for the purpose of improving staff relations and of handling grievances, it is BEST that these meetings be held

    A. at regular intervals
    B. whenever requested by an aggrieved employee
    C. at the discretion of the administrative officer
    D. whenever the need arises

3._____

4. In the theory and practice of public administration, the one of the following which is LEAST generally regarded as a staff function is

    A. budgeting
    C. purchasing
    B. fire fighting
    D. research and information

4._____

5. The LEAST essential factor in the successful application of a service rating system is

    A. careful training of reporting officers
    B. provision for self-rating
    C. statistical analysis to check reliability
    D. utilization of objective standards of performance

5._____

6. Of the following, the one which is NOT an aim of service rating plans is   6._____

    A. establishment of a fair method of measuring employee value to the employer
    B. application of a uniform measurement to employees of the same class and grade performing similar functions
    C. application of a uniform measurement to employees of the same class and grade however different their assignments may be
    D. establishment of a scientific duties plan

7. A rule or regulation relating to the internal management of a department becomes effec-   7._____
tive

    A. only after it is filed in the office of the clerk
    B. as soon as issued by the department head
    C. only after it has been published officially
    D. when approved by the mayor

8. Of the following, the one MOST generally regarded as an *administrative* power is the   8._____

    A. veto power   B. message power
    C. power of pardon   D. rule making power

9. In public administration functional allocation involves   9._____

    A. integration and the assignment of administrative power
    B. the assignment of a single power to a single administrative level
    C. the distribution of a number of subsidiary responsibilities among all levels of government
    D. decentralization of administrative responsibilities

10. In the field of public administration, the LEAST general result of coordination is the   10._____

    A. performance of a well–rounded job
    B. elimination of jurisdictional overlapping
    C. performance of functions otherwise neglected
    D. elimination of duplication of work

11. Of the following, the MOST complicated and difficult problem confronting the reorganizer   11._____
in the field of public administration is

    A. ridding the government of graft
    B. ridding the government of crude incompetence
    C. ridding the government of excessive decentralization
    D. conditioning organization to modern social and economic life

12. The *most accurate* description of the process of integration in the field of public adminis-   12._____
tration is

    A. transfer of administrative authority from a lower to a higher level of government
    B. transfer of administrative authority from a higher to a lower level of government
    C. concentration of administrative authority within one level of government
    D. formal cooperation between city and state governments to administer a function

13. The one of the following who was *most closely* allied with *scientific management* is   13.____

     A.   Mosher   B.   Probst   C.   Taylor   D.   White

14. Of the following wall colors, the one which will reflect the GREATEST amount of light,   14.____
other things being equal, is

     A.   buff   B.   light gray   C.   light blue   D.   brown

15. Natural illumination is LEAST necessary in a(n)   15.____

     A.   executive office   B.   reception room
     C.   central stenographic bureau   D.   conference room

16. The MOST desirable relative humidity in an office is   16.____

     A.   30%   B.   50%   C.   70%   D.   90%

17. When several pieces of correspondence are filed in the same folder they are *usually*   17.____
arranged

     A.   according to subject   B.   numerically
     C.   in the order in which they are received   D.   alphabetically

18. Eliminating slack in work assignments is   18.____

     A.   speed-up   B.   time study   C.   motion study
     D.   efficient managment

19. *Time studies* examine and measure   19.____

     A.   past performance   B.   present performance
     C.   long-run effect   D.   influence of change

20. In making a position analysis for a duties classification, the one of the following factors   20.____
which must be considered is the

     A.   capabilities of the incumbent
     B.   qualifications of the incumbent
     C.   efficiency attained by the incumbent
     D.   responsibility assigned to the incumbent

21. The MAXIMUM number of subordinates who can be effectively supervised by one   21.____
administrative assistant is BEST considered as

     A.   determined by the law of *span of control*
     B.   determined by the law of *span of attention*
     C.   determined by the type of work supervised
     D.   fixed at not more than six

22. Of the following devices used in personnel administration, the MOST basic is   22.____

     A.   classification   B.   service rating
     C.   appeals   D.   in-service training

23. Of the following, the LEAST important factor for sound organization is the   23.____

    A. individual and his position
    B. hierarchical form of organization
    C. location and delegation of authority
    D. standardization of salary schedules

24. *Stretch–out* is a term that originated with the   24.____

    A. imposition of a furlough
    B. system of semi–monthly relief payments
    C. development of labor technology
    D. irregular development of low–cost housing projects

25. The one of the following which is LEAST generally true of a personnel division in a large   25.____
department is that it is

    A. concerned with having a certain point of view on personnel permeate the executive staff
    B. charged with aiding operating executives with auxiliary staff service, assistance and advice
    C. charged to administer a certain few operating duties of its own
    D. charged with the basic responsibility for the efficient operation of the entire department

_____

KEY (CORRECT ANSWERS)

1.	A		11.	D
2.	C		12.	C
3.	A		13.	C
4.	B		14.	A
5.	B		15.	B
6.	D		16.	A
7.	B		17.	C
8.	D		18.	D
9.	C		19.	B
10.	C		20.	D

21.	C
22.	A
23.	D
24.	C
25.	D

TEST 2

Questions 1-10.

DIRECTIONS: Below are ten words numbered 1 through 10 and twenty other words divided into four groups - Group A, Group B, Group C and Group D. For each of the ten numbered words, select the word in one of the four groups which is MOST NEARLY the same in meaning. The letter of that group is the answer for the item. *PRINT THE LETTER OF THE CORRECT ANSWER IN THE SPACE AT THE RIGHT.*

1. abnegation	GROUP A	GROUP B	GROUP C	1.____
2. calumnious	articulation	bituminous	assumption	2.____
	fusion	deductive	forecast	
3. purview	catastrophic	repudiation	terse	3.____
	inductive	doleful	insolence	
4. lugubrious	leadership	prolonged	panorama	4.____
5. hegemony				5.____
6. arrogation		GROUP D		6.____
7. coalescence		scope		7.____
		vindication		
8. prolix		amortization		8.____
		productive		
9. syllogistic		slanderous		9.____
10. contumely				10.____

Questions 11-25.

DIRECTIONS: Each question or incomplete statement is followed by several suggested answers or completions. Select the one that BEST answers the question or completes the statement.

11. In large cities the total cost of government is of course *greater* than in small cities but   11.____

    A.   this is accompanied by a decrease in per capita cost
    B.   the per capita cost is also greater
    C.   the per capita cost is approximately the same
    D.   the per capita cost is considerably less in approximately 50% of the cases

12. The one of the following which is LEAST characteristic of governmental reorganizations   12.____
    is the

    A.   saving of large sums of money
    B.   problem of morale and personnel
    C.   task of logic and management
    D.   engineering approach

13. The LEAST accurate of the following statements about graphic presentation is 13.____

    A. it is desirable to show as many coordinate lines as possible in a finished diagram
    B. the horizontal scale should read from left to right and the vertical scale from top to bottom
    C. when two or more curves are represented for comparison on the same chart, their zero lines should coincide
    D. a percentage curve should not be used when the purpose is to show the actual amounts of increase or decrease

14. Grouping of figures in a frequency distribution results in a *loss* of 14.____

    A. linearity   B. significance   C. detail   D. coherence

15. The true financial condition of a city is BEST reflected when its accounting system is placed upon a(n) 15.____

    A. cash basis   B. accrual basis
    C. fiscal basis   D. warrant basis

16. When the discrepancy between the totals of a trial balance is $36, the LEAST probable cause of the error is 16.____

    A. omission of an item
    B. entering of an item on the wrong side of the ledger
    C. a mistake in addition or subtraction
    D. transposition of digits

17. For the *most effective* administrative management, appropriations should be 17.____

    A. itemized   B. lump sum   C. annual   D. bi-annual

18. Of the following types of expenditure control in the practice of fiscal management, the one which is LEAST important is that which relates to 18.____

    A. past policy affecting expenditures
    B. future policy affecting expenditures
    C. prevention of improper use of funds
    D. prevention of overdraft

19. The sinking fund method of retiring bonds does NOT 19.____

    A. permit investment in a new issue of city bonds when the general market is unsatisfactory
    B. cause irreparable injury to the city's credit when the city is unable to make a scheduled contribution
    C. require periodic actuarial computations
    D. cost as much to administer as the serial bond method

20. Of the following, the statement that is FALSE is: 20.____

    A.   Non-profit hospitalization plans are based on underlying principles similar to those which underlie mutual insurance

    B.   Federal, state and local governments pay for more than half of the medical care received by more than half of the population of the country

    C.   In addition to non-profit hospitalization, non-profit organizations providing reimbursement for medical and nursing care are now being organized in this state

    D.   Voluntary health insurance must be depended on since a state system of health insurance is unconstitutional

21. The *most accurate* of the following statements concerning birth and death rates is: 21.____

    A.   A high birth rate is usually accompanied by a relatively high death rate

    B.   A high birth rate is usually accompanied by a relatively low death rate

    C.   The rate of increase in population for a given area may be obtained by subtracting the death rate from the birth rate

    D.   The rate of increase in population for a given area may be obtained by subtracting the birth rate from the death rate

22. Empirical reasoning is based upon   22.____

    A.   experience and observation

    B.   *a priori* propositions

    C.   application of an established generalization

    D.   logical deduction

23. 45% of the employees of a certain department are enrolled in in-service training courses   23.____
and 35% are registered in college courses.
The percentage of employees NOT enrolled in either of these types of courses is

    A. 20%   B. at least 20% and not more than 55%

    C. approximately 40%   D. none of these

24. A typist can address approximately R envelopes in a 7-hour day. A list containing S   24.____
addresses is submitted with a request that all envelopes be typed within T hours.
The number of typists needed to complete this task would be

    A. $\dfrac{7RS}{T}$ B. $\dfrac{S}{7RT}$ C. $\dfrac{R}{7ST}$ D. $\dfrac{7S}{RT}$

25. Bank X allows a customer to write without charge five checks per month for each $100   25.____
on deposit, but a check deposited or a cash deposit counts the same as a check written.
Bank Y charges ten cents for every check written, requires no minimum balance and
allows deposit of cash or of checks made out to customer free. A man receives two salary checks and, on the average, five other checks each month. He pays, on the average,
twelve bills a month, five of which are for amounts between $5 and $10, five for amounts
between $10 and $20, two for about $30. Assume that he pays these bills either by check
or by Post Office money order (the charges for money orders are: $3.01 to $10–11¢;
$10.01 to $20–13¢; $20.01 to $40–15¢) and that he has a savings account paying 2%.
Assume also that if he has an account at Bank X, he keeps a balance sufficient to avoid
any service charges. Of the following statements in relation to this man, the one that is
TRUE is that

    A. the monthly cost of an account at Bank Y is approximately as great as the cost of
an account at Bank X and also the account is more convenient
    B. to use an account at Bank Y costs more than the use of money orders, but this dis-
advantage is offset by the fact that cancelled checks act as receipts for bills paid
    C. money orders are cheapest but this advantage is offset by the fact that one must
go to the Post Office for each order
    D. an account at Bank X is least expensive and has the advantage that checks
endorsed to the customer may be deposited in it

———

KEY (CORRECT ANSWERS)

1.	B		11.	B
2.	D		12.	A
3.	D		13.	A
4.	B		14.	C
5.	A		15.	B
6.	C		16.	C
7.	A		17.	B
8.	B		18.	A
9.	B		19.	B
10.	C		20.	D

21.	A
22.	A
23.	B
24.	D
25.	D

———

EXAMINATION SECTION
TEST 1

DIRECTIONS: Each question or incomplete statement is followed by several suggested answers or completions. Select the one that BEST answers the question or completes the statement. *PRINT THE LETTER OF THE CORRECT ANSWER IN THE SPACE AT THE RIGHT.*

1. A management approach widely used today is based on the belief that decisions should be made and actions should be taken by managers closest to the organization's problems.
    This style of management is MOST appropriately called _____ management.

      A. scientific
      C. decentralized
      B. means-end
      D. internal process

1.____

2. As contrasted with tall organization structures with narrow spans of control, flat organization structures with wide spans of control MOST usually provide

      A. fast communication and information flows
      B. more levels in the organizational hierarchy
      C. fewer workers reporting to supervisors
      D. lower motivation because of tighter control standards

2.____

3. Use of the systems approach is MOST likely to lead to

      A. consideration of the impact on the whole organization of actions taken in any part of that organization
      B. the placing of restrictions on departmental authority
      C. use of mathematical models to suboptimize production
      D. consideration of the activities of each unit of an organization as a totality without regard to the remainder of the organization

3.____

4. An administrator, with overall responsibility for all administrative operations in a large operating agency, is considering organizing the agency's personnel office around either of the following two alternative concepts:
    Alternative I-   a corps of specialists for each branch of personnel subject matter, whose skills, counsel, or work products are coordinated only by the agency personnel officer
    Alternative II-   a crew of so-called *personnel generalists,* who individually work with particular segments of the organization but deal with all subspecialties of the personnel function
    The one of the following which MOST tends to be a DRAWBACK of Alternative I, as compared with Alternative II, is that

      A. training and employee relations work call for education, interests, and talents that differ from those required for classification and compensation work
      B. personnel office staff may develop only superficial familiarity with the specialized areas to which they have been assigned
      C. supervisors may fail to get continuing overall personnel advice on an integrated basis
      D. the personnel specialists are likely to become so interested in and identified with the operating view as to particular cases that they lose their professional objectivity and become merely advocates of what some supervisor wants

4.____

5. The matrix summary or decision matrix is a useful tool for making choices. Its effectiveness is MOST dependent upon the user's ability to

    A. write a computer program (Fortran or Cobol)
    B. assign weights representing the relative importance of the objectives
    C. solve a set of two equations with two unknowns
    D. work with matrix algebra

5._____

6. An organizational form which is set up only on an *ad hoc* basis to meet specific goals is said PRIMARILY to use

    A. clean break departmentation
    B. matrix or task force organization
    C. scalar specialization
    D. geographic or area-wide decentralization

6._____

7. The concept of job enlargement would LEAST properly be implemented by

    A. permitting workers to follow through on tasks or projects from start to finish
    B. delegating the maximum authority possible for decision-making to lower levels in the hierarchy
    C. maximizing the number of professional classes in the classification plan
    D. training employees to grow beyond whatever tasks they have been performing

7._____

8. As used in the area of administration, the principle of *unity of command* MOST specifically means that

    A. an individual should report to only one superior for any single activity
    B. individuals make better decisions than do committees
    C. in large organizations, chains of command are normally too long
    D. an individual should not supervise over five subordinates

8._____

9. The methods of operations research, statistical decision-making, and linear programming have been referred to as the tool kit of the manager.
Utilization of these tools is LEAST useful in the performance of which of the following functions?

    A. Elimination of the need for using judgment when making decisions
    B. Facilitation of decision-making without the need for sub-optimization
    C. Quantifying problems for management study
    D. Research and analysis of management operations

9._____

10. When acting in their respective managerial capacities, the chief executive officer and the office supervisor both perform the fundamental functions of management. Of the following differences between the two, the one which is generally considered to be the LEAST significant is the

    A. breadth of the objectives
    B. complexity of measuring actual efficiency of performance
    C. number of decisions made
    D. organizational relationships affected by actions taken

10._____

11. The ability of operations researchers to solve complicated problems rests on their use of models.
    These models can BEST be described as

    A. mathematical statements of the problem
    B. physical constructs that simulate a work layout
    C. toy-like representations of employees in work environments
    D. role-playing simulations

11.____

12. Of the following, it is MOST likely to be proper for the agency head to allow the agency personnel officer to make final selection of appointees from certified eligible lists where there are

    A. *small* numbers of employees to be hired in newly-developed professional fields
    B. *large* numbers of persons to be hired for key managerial positions
    C. *large* numbers of persons to be hired in very routine occupations where the individual discretion of operating officials is not vital
    D. *small* numbers of persons to be hired in highly specialized professional occupations which are vital to the agency's operations

12.____

13. Of the following, an operating agency personnel office is LEAST likely to be able to exert strong influence or control within the operating agency by

    A. interpreting to the operating agency head what is intended by the directives and rules emanating from the central personnel agency
    B. establishing the key objectives of those line divisions of the operating agency employing large numbers of staff and operating under the management-by-objectives approach
    C. formulating and proposing to the agency head the internal policies and procedures on personnel matters required within the operating agency
    D. exercising certain discretionary authority in the application of the agency head's general personnel policies to actual specific situations

13.____

14. PERT is a recently developed system used *primarily* to

    A. evaluate the quality of applicants' backgrounds
    B. analyze and control the timing aspects of a major project
    C. control the total expenditure of agency funds within a monthly or quarterly time period
    D. analyze and control the differential effect on costs of purchasing in different quantities

14.____

15. Assume that an operating agency has among its vacant positions two positions, each of which encompasses mixed duties. Both require appointees to have considerable education and experience, but these requirements are essential only for the more difficult duties of these positions. In the place of these positions, an administrator creates two new positions, one in which the higher duties are concentrated and the other with the lesser functions requiring only minimum preparation.
    Of the following, it is generally MOST appropriate to characterize the administrator's action as a(n)

15.____

A. *undesirable* example of deliberate downgrading of standards and requirements
B. *undesirable* manipulation of the classification system for non-merit purposes
C. *desirable* broadening of the definition of a class of positions
D. *desirable* example of job redesign

16. Of the following, the LEAST important stumbling block to the development of personnel mobility among governmental jurisdictions is the

16.____

    A. limitations on lateral entry above junior levels in many jurisdictions
    B. continued collection of filing fees for civil service tests by many governmental jurisdictions
    C. absence of reciprocal exchange of retirement benefit eligibility between governments
    D. disparities in salary scales between governments

17. Of the following, the MAJOR disadvantage of a personnel system that features the *selection out* (forced retirement) of those who have been passed over a number of times for promotion is that such a system

17.____

    A. wastes manpower which is perfectly competent at one level but unable to rise above that level
    B. wastes funds by requiring review boards
    C. leads to excessive recruiting of newcomers from outside the system
    D. may not be utilized in *closed* career systems with low maximum age limits for entrance

18. Of the following, the fields in which operating agency personnel offices generally exercise the MOST stringent controls over first line supervisors in the agency are

18.____

    A. methods analysis and work simplification
    B. selection and position classification
    C. vestibule training and Gantt chart
    D. suggestion systems and staff development

19. Of the following, computers are normally MOST effective in handling

19.____

    A. large masses of data requiring simple processing
    B. small amounts of data requiring constantly changing complex processing
    C. data for which reported values are often subject to inaccuracies
    D. large amounts of data requiring continual programming and reprocessing

20. Contingency planning, which has long been used by the military and is assuming increasing importance in other organizations, may BEST be described as a process which utilizes

20.____

    A. alternative plans based on varying assumptions
    B. *crash programs* by organizations departmentalized along process lines
    C. plans which mandate substitution of equipment for manpower at predetermined operational levels
    D. plans that individually and accurately predict future events

21. In the management of inventory, two kinds of costs normally determine when to order and in what amounts. The one of the following choices which includes BOTH of these kinds of costs is _____ costs and _____ costs.

    A. carrying; storage   B. personnel; order
    C. computer; order   D. personnel; computer

21.____

22. At top management levels, the one of the following which is generally the MOST important executive skill is skill in

    A. budgeting procedures
    B. a technical discipline
    C. controlling actions in accordance with previously approved plans
    D. seeing the organization as a whole

22.____

23. Of the following, the BEST way to facilitate the successful operation of a committee is to set guidelines establishing its

    A. budget exclusive of personnel costs
    B. location
    C. schedule of meetings or conferences
    D. scope or purpose

23.____

24. Executive training programs that single out particular managers and groom them for promotion create the so-called organizational *crown princes.*
Of the following, the MOST serious problem that arises in connection with this practice is that

    A. the managers chosen for promotion seldom turn out to be the best managers since the future potential of persons cannot be predicted
    B. not enough effort is made to remove organizational obstacles in the way of their development and achievement
    C. the resentment of the managers not selected for the program has an adverse effect on the motivation of those managers not selected
    D. performance appraisal and review are not carried out systematically enough

24.____

25. Of the following, the LEAST likely result of the use of the concept of job enlargement is that

    A. coordination will be simplified
    B. the individual's job will become less challenging
    C. worker satisfaction will increase
    D. fewer people will have to give attention to each piece of work

25.____

KEY (CORRECT ANSWERS)

1.	C		11.	A
2.	A		12.	C
3.	A		13.	B
4.	C		14.	B
5.	B		15.	D
6.	B		16.	B
7.	C		17.	A
8.	A		18.	B
9.	A		19.	A
10.	C		20.	A

21.	A
22.	D
23.	D
24.	C
25.	B

TEST 2

DIRECTIONS: Each question or incomplete statement is followed by several suggested answers or completions. Select the one that BEST answers the question or completes the statement. *PRINT THE LETTER OF THE CORRECT ANSWER IN THE SPACE AT THE RIGHT.*

1. The one of the following which is MOST likely to be emphasized in the use of the brainstorming technique is the   1.____

   A. early consideration of cost factors of all ideas which may be suggested
   B. avoidance of impractical suggestions
   C. separation of the generation of ideas from their evaluation
   D. appraisal of suggestions concurrently with their initial presentation

2. Of the following, the BEST method for assessing managerial performance is generally to   2.____

   A. compare the manager's accomplishments against clear, specific, agreed-upon goals
   B. compare the manager's traits with those of his peers on a predetermined objective scale
   C. measure the manager's behavior against a listing of itemized personal traits
   D. measure the manager's success according to the enumeration of the *satisfaction* principle

3. As compared with recruitment from outside, selection from within the service must generally show GREATER concern for the   3.____

   A. prestige in which the public service as a whole is held by the public
   B. morale of the candidate group comprising the recruitment field
   C. cost of examining per candidate
   D. benefits of the use of standardized and validated tests

4. Performance budgeting focuses PRIMARY attention upon which one of the following? The   4.____

   A. things to be acquired, such as supplies and equipment
   B. general character and relative importance of the work to be done or the service to be rendered
   C. list of personnel to be employed, by specific title
   D. separation of employee performance evaluations from employee compensation

5. Of the following, the FIRST step in the installation and operation of a performance budgeting system generally should be the   5.____

   A. identification of program costs in relationship to the accounting system and operating structure
   B. identification of the specific end results of past programs in other jurisdictions
   C. identification of work programs that are meaningful for management purposes
   D. establishment of organizational structures each containing only one work program

6. Of the following, the MOST important purpose of a system of quarterly allotments of appropriated funds generally is to enable the

    6.____

   A. head of the judicial branch to determine the legality of agency requests for budget increases
   B. operating agencies of government to upgrade the quality of their services without increasing costs
   C. head of the executive branch to control the rate at which the operating agencies obligate and expend funds
   D. operating agencies of government to avoid payment for services which have not been properly rendered by employees

7. In the preparation of the agency's budget, the agency's central budget office has two responsibilities: program review and management improvement.
Which one of the following questions concerning an operating agency's program is MOST closely related to the agency budget officer's program review responsibility?

    7.____

   A. Can expenditures for supplies, materials, or equipment be reduced?
   B. Will improved work methods contribute to a more effective program?
   C. What is the relative importance of this program as compared with other programs?
   D. Will a realignment of responsibilities contribute to a higher level of program performance?

8. Of the following, the method of evaluating relative rates of return normally and generally thought to be MOST useful in evaluating government operations is _____ analysis.

    8.____

   A. cost-benefit   B. budget variance
   C. investment capital   D. budget planning program

9. The one of the following assumptions that is LEAST likely to be made by a democratic or permissive type of leader is that

    9.____

   A. commitment to goals is seldom a result of monetary rewards alone
   B. people can learn not only to accept, but also to seek, responsibility
   C. the average person prefers security over advancement
   D. creativity may be found in most segments of the population

10. In attempting to motivate subordinates, a manager should PRINCIPALLY be aware of the fact that

    10.____

   A. the psychological qualities of people, in general, are easily predictable
   B. fear, as a traditional form of motivation, has lost much of its former power to motivate people in our modern industrial society
   C. fear is still the most potent force in motivating the behavior of subordinates in the public service
   D. the worker has very little control over the quality and quantity of his output

11. Assume that the following figures represent the number of work-units that were produced   11.____
during a week by each of sixteen employees in a division:

12	16	13	18
21	12	16	13
16	13	17	21
13	15	18	20

If all of the employees of the division who produced thirteen work-units during the
week had instead produced fifteen work-units during that same week, then for that
week, the

   A. mean, median, and mode would all change
   B. mean and mode would change, but the median would remain the same
   C. mode and median would change, but the mean would remain the same
   D. mode, mean, and median would all still remain unchanged in value

12. An important law in motivation theory is called the *law of effect.* This law says that behav-   12.____
ior which satisfies a person's needs tends to be repeated; behavior which does not satisfy a person's needs tends to be eliminated. The one of the following which is the BEST
interpretation of this law is that

   A. productivity depends on personality traits
   B. diversity of goals leads to instability of motivation
   C. the greater the satisfaction, the more likely it is that the behavior will be reinforced
   D. extrinsic satisfaction is more important than intrinsic reward

13. Of the following, the MOST acceptable reason an administrator can give for taking advice   13.____
from other employees in the organization only when he asks for it is that he wants to

   A. encourage creativity and high morale
   B. keep dysfunctional pressures and inconsistent recommendations to a minimum
   C. show his superiors and peers who is in charge
   D. show his subordinates who is in charge

14. A complete picture of the communication channels in an organization can BEST be   14.____
revealed by

   A. observing the planned paperwork system
   B. recording the highly intermittent patterns of communication
   C. plotting the entire flow of information over a period of time
   D. monitoring the *grapevine*

Questions 15-16.

DIRECTIONS: Answer Questions 15 and 16 SOLELY on the basis of the passage below.

Management by objectives (MBO) may be defined as the process by which the superior and the subordinate managers of an organization jointly define its common goals, define each individual's major areas of responsibility in terms of the results expected of him and use these measures as guides for operating the unit and assessing the contribution of each of its members.

The MBO approach requires that after organizational goals are established and communicated, targets must be set for each individual position which are congruent with organizational goals. Periodic performance reviews and a final review using the objectives set as criteria are also basic to this approach.

Recent studies have shown that MBO programs are influenced by attitudes and perceptions of the boss, the company, the reward-punishment system, and the program itself. In addition, the manner in which the MBO program is carried out can influence the success of the program. A study done in the late sixties indicates that the best results are obtained when the manager sets goals which deal with significant problem areas in the organizational unit, or with the subordinate's personal deficiencies. These goals must be clear with regard to what is expected of the subordinate. The frequency of feedback is also important in the success of a management-by-Objectives program. Generally, the greater the amount of feedback, the more successful the MBO program.

15. According to the above passage, the expected output for individual employees should be   15._____
     determined

     A.   after a number of reviews of work performance
     B.   after common organizational goals are defined
     C.   before common organizational goals are defined
     D.   on the basis of an employee's personal qualities

16. According to the above passage, the management-by-objectives approach requires   16._____

     A.   less feedback than other types of management programs
     B.   little review of on-the-job performance after the initial setting of goals
     C.   general conformance between individual goals and organizational goals
     D.   the setting of goals which deal with minor problem areas in the organization

Questions 17-19.

DIRECTIONS: Answer Questions 17 to 19 SOLELY on the basis of the passage below.

During the last decade, a great deal of interest has been generated around the phenomenon of organizational development, or the process of developing human resources through conscious organisation effort. Organizational development (OD) stresses improving interpersonal relationships and organizational skills, such as communication, to a much greater degree than individual training ever did.

The kind of training that an organization should emphasize depends upon the present and future structure of the organization. If future organizations are to be unstable, shifting coalitions, then individual skills and abilities, particularly those emphasizing innovativeness, creativity, flexibility, and the latest technological knowledge, are crucial, and individual training is most appropriate.

But if there is to be little change in organizational structure, then the main thrust of training should be group-oriented or organizational development. This approach seems better designed for overcoming hierarchical barriers, for developing a degree of interpersonal relationships which make communication along the chain of command possible, and for retaining a modicum of innovation and/or flexibility.

17. According to the above passage, group-oriented training is MOST useful in

    A. developing a communications system that will facilitate understanding through the chain of command
    B. highly flexible and mobile organizations
    C. preventing the crossing of hierarchical barriers within an organization
    D. saving energy otherwise wasted on developing methods of dealing with rigid hierarchies

17.____

18. The one of the following conclusions which can be drawn MOST appropriately from the above passage is that

    A. behavioral research supports the use of organizational development training methods rather than individualized training
    B. it is easier to provide individualized training in specific skills than to set up sensitivity training programs
    C. organizational development eliminates innovative or flexible activity
    D. the nature of an organization greatly influences which training methods will be most effective

18.____

19. According to the above passage, the one of the following which is LEAST important for large-scale organizations geared to rapid and abrupt change is

    A. current technological information
    B. development of a high degree of interpersonal relationships
    C. development of individual skills and abilities
    D. emphasis on creativity

19.____

Questions 20-25.

DIRECTIONS: Each of Questions 20 through 25 consists of a statement which contains one word that is incorrectly used because it is not in keeping with the meaning that the quotation is evidently intended to convey. Determine which word is INCORRECTLY used. Select from the choices lettered A, B, C, and D the word which, when substituted for the incorrectly used word, would BEST help to convey the meaning of the statement.

20. One of the considerations likely to affect the currency of classification, particularly in pro-   20.____
fessional and managerial occupations, is the impact of the incumbent's capacities on the
job. Some work is highly susceptible to change as the result of the special talents or
interests of the classifier. Organization should never be so rigid as not to capitalize on the
innovative or unusual proclivities of its key employees. While a machine operator may not
be able, even subtly, to change the character or level of his job, the design engineer, the
attorney, or the organization and methods analyst might readily do so. Reliance on his
judgment and the scope of his assignments may both grow as the result of his skill,
insight, and capacity.

   A. unlikely   B. incumbent   C. directly   D. scope

21. The supply of services by the state is not governed by market price. The aim is to supply   21.____
such services to all who need them and to treat all consumers equally. This objective
especially compels the civil servant to maintain a role of strict impartiality, based on the
principle of equality of individual citizens vis-a-vis their government. However, there is a
clear difference between being neutral and being impartial. If the requirement is construed to mean that all civil servants should be political eunuchs, devoid of the drive and
motivation essential to dynamic administration, then the concept of impartiality is being
seriously utilized. Modern governments should not be stopped from demanding that their
hirelings have not only the technical but the emotional qualifications necessary for whole-
hearted effort.

   A. determined   B. rule   C. stable   D. misapplied

22. The manager was barely listening. Recently, at the divisional level, several new fronts of   22.____
troubles had erupted, including a requirement to increase production yet hold down operating costs and somehow raise quality standards. Though the three objectives were basically obsolete, top departmental management was insisting on the simultaneous
attainment of them, an insistence not helping the manager's ulcer, an old enemy within.
Thus, the manager could not find time for interest in individuals-only in statistics which
regiments of individuals, like unconsidered Army privates, added up to.

   A. quantity   B. battalion   C. incompatible   D. quiet

23. When a large volume of data flows directly between operators and first-line supervisors,   23.____
senior executives tend to be out of the mainstream of work. Summary reports can
increase their remoteness. An executive needs to know the volume, quality, and cost of
completed work, and exceptional problems. In addition, he may desire information on key
operating conditions. Summary reports on these matters are, therefore, essential features of a communications network and make delegation without loss of control possible.

   A. unimportant   B. quantity
   C. offset   D. incomplete

24. Of major significance in management is harmony between the overall objectives of the organization and the managerial objectives within that organization. In addition, harmony among goals of managers is impossible; they should not be at cross-purposes. Each manager's goal should supplement and assist the goals of his colleagues. Likewise, the objectives of individuals or nonmanagement members should be harmonized with those of the manager. When this is accomplished, genuine teamwork is the result, and human relations are aided materially. The integration of managers' and individuals' goals aids in achieving greater work satisfaction at all levels.

24.____

    A. competition   B. dominate
    C. incremental   D. vital

25. Change constantly challenges the manager. Some of this change is evolutionary, some revolutionary, some recognizable, some nonrecognizable. Both forces within an enterprise and forces outside the enterprise cause managers to act and react in initiating changes in their immediate working environment. Change invalidates existing operations. Goals are not being accomplished in the best manner, problems develop, and frequently because of the lack of time, only patched-up solutions are followed. The result is that the mode of management is profound in nature and temporary in effectiveness. A complete overhaul of managerial operations should take place. It appears quite likely that we are just beginning to see the real effects of change in our society; the pace probably will accelerate in ways that few really understand or know how to handle.

25.____

    A. confirms   B. decline
    C. instituting   D. superficial

KEY (CORRECT ANSWERS)

1.	C	11.	B
2.	A	12.	C
3.	B	13.	B
4.	B	14.	C
5.	C	15.	B
6.	C	16.	C
7.	C	17.	A
8.	A	18.	D
9.	C	19.	B
10.	B	20.	B

21.	D
22.	C
23.	C
24.	D
25.	D

EXAMINATION SECTION
TEST 1

DIRECTIONS: Each question or incomplete statement is followed by several suggested answers or completions. Select the one that BEST answers the question or completes the statement. *PRINT THE LETTER OF THE CORRECT ANSWER IN THE SPACE AT THE RIGHT.*

1. Assume that a manager is preparing a list of reasons to justify making a major change in methods and procedures in his agency.
   Which of the following reasons would be LEAST appropriate on such a list?

   A. Improve the means for satisfying needs and wants of agency personnel
   B. Increase efficiency
   C. Intensify competition and stimulate loyalty to separate work groups
   D. Contribute to the individual and group satisfaction of agency personnel

   1.____

2. Many managers recognize the benefits of decentralization but are concerned about the danger of over-relaxation of control as a result of increased delegation.
   Of the following, the MOST appropriate means of establishing proper control under decentralization is for the manager to

   A. establish detailed standards for all phases of operation
   B. shift his attention from operating details to appraisal of results
   C. keep himself informed by decreasing the time span covered by reports
   D. make unilateral decisions on difficult situations that arise in decentralized locations

   2.____

3. In some agencies, the counsel to the agency head is given the right to bypass the chain of command and issue orders directly to the staff concerning matters that involve certain specific processes and practices.
   This situation MOST NEARLY illustrates the principle of

   A. the acceptance theory of authority
   B. multiple-linear authority
   C. splintered authority
   D. functional authority

   3.____

4. Assume that a manager is writing a brief report to his superior outlining the advantages of matrix organization. Of the following, it would be INCORRECT to state that

   A. in matrix organization, a project is emphasized by designating one individual as the focal point for all matters pertaining to it
   B. utilization of manpower can be flexible in matrix organization because a reservoir of specialists is maintained in the line operations
   C. the usual line staff arrangement is generally reversed in matrix organization
   D. in matrix organization, responsiveness to project needs is generally faster due to establishing needed communication lines and decision points

   4.____

5. It is commonly understood that communication is an important part of the administrative process.
Which of the following is NOT a valid principle of the communication process in administration?

    A. The channels of communication should be spontaneous.
    B. The lines of communication should be as direct and as short as possible.
    C. Communications should be authenticated.
    D. The persons serving in communications centers should be competent.

5.____

6. The PRIMARY purpose of the quantitative approach in management is to

    A. identify better alternatives for management decision-making
    B. substitute data for judgment
    C. match opinions to data
    D. match data to opinions

6.____

7. If an executive wants to make a strong case for running his agency as a flat type of structure, he should point out that the PRIMARY advantage of doing so is to

    A. provide less experience in decision-making for agency personnel
    B. facilitate frequent contact between each superior and his immediate subordinates
    C. improve communication and unify attitudes
    D. improve communication and diversify attitudes

7.____

8. In deciding how detailed his delegation of authority to a subordinate should be, a manager should follow the general principle that

    A. delegation of authority is more detailed at the top of the organizational structure
    B. detailed delegation of authority is associated with detailed work assignments
    C. delegation of authority should be in sufficient detail to prevent overlapping assignments
    D. detailed delegation of authority is associated with broad work assignments

8.____

9. In recent years, newer and more fluid types of organizational forms have been developed. One of these is a type of free-form organization.
Another name for this type of organization is the

    A. project organization
    B. semimix organization
    C. naturalistic structure
    D. semipermanent structure

9.____

10. Which of the following is the MAJOR objective of operational or management systems audits?

    A. Determining the number of personnel needed
    B. Recommending opportunities for improving operating and management practices
    C. Detecting fraud
    D. Determining organization problems

10.____

11. Assume that a manager observes that conflict exists between his agency and another operating agency of government.
Which of the following statements is the LEAST probable cause of this conflict?

    A. Incompatibility between the agencies' goals but similarity in their resource allocations
    B. Compatibility between agencies' goals and resources
    C. Status differences between agency personnel
    D. Differences in perceptions of each other's policies

11.____

12. Of the following, a MAJOR purpose of brainstorming as a problem-solving technique is to

    A. develop the ability to concentrate
    B. encourage creative thinking
    C. evaluate employees' ideas
    D. develop critical ability

12.____

13. The one of the following requirements which is LEAST likely to accompany regular delegation of work from a manager to a subordinate is a(n)

    A. need to review the organization's workload
    B. indication of what work the subordinate is to do
    C. need to grant authority to the subordinate
    D. obligation for the subordinate who accepts the work to try to complete it

13.____

14. Of the following, the one factor which is generally considered LEAST essential to successful committee operation is

    A. stating a clear definition of the authority and scope of the committee
    B. selecting the committee chairman carefully
    C. limiting the size of the committee to four persons
    D. limiting the subject matter to that which can be handled in group discussion

14.____

15. In using the program evaluation and review technique, the *critical path* is the path that

    A. requires the shortest time
    B. requires the longest time
    C. focuses most attention on social constraints
    D. focuses most attention on repetitious jobs

15.____

16. Which one of the following is LEAST characteristic of the management-by-objectives approach?

    A. The scope within which the employee may exercise decision-making is broadened
    B. The employee starts with a self-appraisal of his performances, abilities, and potential
    C. Emphasis is placed on activities performed; activities orientation is maximized
    D. Each employee participates in determining his own objectives

16.____

17. The function of management which puts into effect the decisions, plans, and programs that have previously been worked out for achieving the goals of the group is MOST appropriately called   17.____

    A. scheduling   B. classifying
    C. budgeting   D. directing

18. In the establishment of a plan to improve office productive efficiency, which of the following guidelines is LEAST helpful in setting sound work standards?   18.____

    A. Employees must accept the plan's objectives.
    B. Current production averages must be promulgated as work standards for a group.
    C. The work flow must generally be fairly constant.
    D. The operation of the plan must be expressed in terms understandable to the worker.

19. The one of the following activities which, generally speaking, is of *relatively* MAJOR importance at the lower-management level and of *somewhat* LESSER importance at higher-management levels is   19.____

    A. actuating   B. forecasting
    C. organizing   D. planning

20. Three styles of leadership exist: democratic, authoritarian, and laissez-faire.   20.____
Of the following work situations, the one in which a democratic approach would normally be the MOST effective is when the work is

    A. routine and moderately complex
    B. repetitious and simple
    C. complex and not routine
    D. simple and not routine

21. Governmental and business organizations *generally* encounter the GREATEST difficulties in developing tangible measures of which one of the following?   21.____

    A. The level of expenditures
    B. Contributions to social welfare
    C. Retention rates
    D. Causes of labor unrest

22. Of the following, a *management-by-objectives* program is BEST described as   22.____

    A. a new comprehensive plan of organization
    B. introduction of budgets and financial controls
    C. introduction of long–range planning
    D. development of future goals with supporting and related progress reviews

23. Research and analysis is probably the most widely used technique for selecting alternatives when major planning decisions are involved.
Of the following, a VALUABLE characteristic of research and analysis is that this technique

    A. places the problem in a meaningful conceptual framework
    B. involves practical application of the various alternatives
    C. accurately analyzes all important tangibles
    D. is much less expensive than other problem–solving methods

23.____

24. If a manager were assigned the task of using a systems approach to designing a new work unit, which of the following should he consider FIRST in carrying out his design?

    A. Networks
    B. Work flows and information processes
    C. Linkages and relationships
    D. Decision points and control loops

24.____

25. The MAIN distinction between Theory X and Theory Y approaches to organization, in accordance with Douglas McGregor's view, is that Theory Y

    A. considers that work is natural to people; Theory X assumes that people are lazy and avoid work
    B. leads to a tall, narrow organization structure, while Theory X leads to one that is flat
    C. organizations motivate people with money; Theory X organizations motivate people with good working conditions
    D. represents authoritarian management, while Theory X management is participative

25.____

———————

KEY (CORRECT ANSWERS)

1.	C	11.	B
2.	B	12.	B
3.	D	13.	A
4.	C	14.	C
5.	A	15.	B
6.	A	16.	C
7.	C	17.	D
8.	B	18.	B
9.	A	19.	A
10.	B	20.	C

21.	B
22.	D
23.	A
24.	B
25.	A

TEST 2

DIRECTIONS: Each question or incomplete statement is followed by several suggested answers or completions. Select the one that BEST answers the question or completes the statement. *PRINT THE LETTER OF THE CORRECT ANSWER IN THE SPACE AT THE RIGHT.*

1. Of the following, the stage in decision-making which is usually MOST difficult is   1.____

    A. stating the alternatives
    B. predicting the possible outcome of each alternative
    C. evaluating the relative merits of each alternative
    D. minimizing the undesirable aspects of the alternative selected

2. In a department where a clerk is reporting both to a senior clerk in charge of the mail   2.____
room and also to a supervising clerk in charge of the duplicating section, there may be a
breakdown of the management principle called

    A. horizontal specialization   B. job enrichment
    C. unity of command   D. Graicunas' Law

3. Of the following, the failure by line managers to accept and appreciate the benefits and   3.____
limitations of a new program or system VERY frequently can be traced to the

    A. budgetary problems involved
    B. resultant need to reduce staff
    C. lack of controls it engenders
    D. failure of top management to support its implementation

4. Although there is general agreement that *management by objectives* has made a major   4.____
contribution to modern management of large organizations, criticisms of the system during the past few years have resulted in

    A. mounting pressure for relaxation of management goals
    B. renewed concern with human values and the manager's personal needs
    C. over-mechanistic application of the perceptions of the behavioral scientists
    D. disillusionment with *management by objectives* on the part of a majority of manag-
        ers

5. Of the following, which is usually considered to be a MAJOR obstacle to the systematic   5.____
analysis of potential problems by managers?

    A. Managers have a tendency to think that all the implications of some proposed step
        cannot be fully understood.
    B. Rewards rarely go to those managers who are most successful at resolving current
        problems in management.
    C. There is a common conviction of managers that their goals are difficult to achieve.
    D. Managers are far more concerned about correcting today's problems than with pre-
        venting tomorrow's.

6. Which of the following should generally have the MOST influence on the selection of supervisors?
6.____

    A. Experience within the work unit where the vacancies exist
    B. Amount of money needed to effect the promotion
    C. Personal preferences of the administration
    D. Evaluation of capacity to exercise supervisory responsibilities

7. In questioning a potential administrator for selection purposes, the one of the following practices which is MOST desirable is to
7.____

    A. encourage the job applicant to give primarily *yes* or *no* replies
    B. get the applicant to talk freely and in detail about his background
    C. let the job applicant speak most of the time
    D. probe the applicant's attitudes, motivation, and willingness to accept responsibility

8. In implementing the managerial function of training subordinates, it is USEFUL to know that a widely agreed–upon definition of human learning is that learning
8.____

    A. is a relatively permanent change in behavior that results from reinforced practice or experience
    B. involves an improvement, but not necessarily a change in behavior
    C. involves a change in behavior, but not necessarily an improvement
    D. is a temporary change in behavior which must be subject to practice or experience

9. If a manager were thinking about using a committee of subordinates to solve an operating problem, which of the following would generally NOT be an advantage of such use of the committee approach?
9.____

    A. Improved coordination   B. Low cost
    C. Increased motivation   D. Integrated judgment

10. Which one of the following management approaches MOST often uses model–building techniques to solve management problems?
    _____ approach
10.____

    A. Behavioral   B. Fiscal
    C. Quantitative   D. Process

11. Of the following, the MOST serious risk in using budgets as a tool for management control is the
11.____

    A. probable neglect of other good management practices
    B. likelihood of guesswork because of the need to plan far in advance
    C. possibility of undue emphasis on factors that are easiest to measure
    D. danger of making qualitative rather than quantitative assessments of performance

12. In government budgeting, the problem of relating financial transactions to the fiscal year in which they are budgeted is BEST met by

    A. determining the cash balance by comparing how much money has been received and how much has been paid out
    B. applying net revenue to the fiscal year in which they are collected as offset by relevant expenses
    C. adopting a system whereby appropriations are entered when they are received and expenditures are entered when they are paid out
    D. entering expenditures on the books when the obligation to make the expenditure is made

12.____

13. If the agency's bookkeeping system records income when it is received and expenditures when the money is paid out, this sytem is USUALLY known as a _____ system.

    A. cash
    B. flow-payment
    C. deferred
    D. fiscal year income

13.____

14. An audit, as the term applies to budget execution, is MOST NEARLY a

    A. procedure based on the budget estimates
    B. control exercised by the executive on the legislature in the establishment of program priorities
    C. check on the legality of expenditures and is based on the appropriations act
    D. requirement which must be met before funds can be spent

14.____

15. In government budgeting, there is a procedure known as *allotment*.
Of the following statements which relate to allotment, select the one that is MOST generally considered to be correct.
Allotment

    A. increases the practice of budget units coming back to the legislative branch for supplemental appropriations
    B. is simply an example of red tape
    C. eliminates the requirement of timing of expenditures
    D. is designed to prevent waste

15.____

16. In government budgeting, the establishment of the schedules of allotments is MOST generally the responsibility of the

    A. budget unit and the legislature
    B. budget unit and the executive
    C. budget unit *only*
    D. executive and the legislature

16.____

17. Of the following statements relating to preparation of an organization's budget request, which is the MOST generally valid precaution?   17.____

    A. Give specific instructions on the format of budget requests and required supporting data
    B. Because of the complexity of preparing a budget request, avoid argumentation to support the requests
    C. Put requests in whatever format is desirable
    D. Consider that final approval will be given to initial estimates

18. Of the following statements which relate to the budget process in a well–organized government, select the one that is MOST NEARLY correct.   18.____

    A. The budget cycle is the step–by–step process which is repeated each and every fiscal year.
    B. Securing approval of the budget does not take place within the budget cycle.
    C. The development of a new budget and putting it into effect is a two–step process known as the budget cycle.
    D. The fiscal period, usually a fiscal year, has no relation to the budget cycle.

19. If a manager were asked what PPBS stands for, he would be RIGHT if he said   19.____

    A. public planning budgeting system
    B. planning programming budgeting system
    C. planning projections budgeting system
    D. programming procedures budgeting system

Questions 20–21.

DIRECTIONS: Answer Questions 20 and 21 on the basis of the following information.

Sample Budget

Refuse Collection	Amount
Personal Services	$ 30,000
Contractual Services	5,000
Supplies and Materials	5,000
Capital Outlay	10,000
	$ 50,000

Residential Collections		
Dwellings–1 pickup per week		1,000
Tons of refuse collected per year		375
Cost of collections per ton	$	8
Cost per dwelling pickup per year	$	3
Total annual cost	$	3,000

20. The sample budget shown is a simplified example of a _____ budget.　　　　20._____

    A.　factorial　　　　　　　　　　　B.　performance
    C.　qualitative　　　　　　　　　　D.　rational

21. The budget shown in the sample differs CHIEFLY from line-item and program budgets in　　21._____
    that it includes

    A.　objects of expenditure but not activities or functions
    B.　only activities, functions, and control
    C.　activities and functions but not objects of expenditures
    D.　levels of service

Question 22.

DIRECTIONS:　Answer Question 22 on the basis of the following information.

Sample Budget

Environmental Safety
    Air Pollution Protection
    Personal Services　　　　　　　　　　　$20,000,000
    Contractual Services　　　　　　　　　　4,000,000
    Supplies and Materials　　　　　　　　　4,000,000
    Capital Outlay　　　　　　　　　　　　2,000,000
       Total Air Pollution Protection　　　　　　　$ 30,000,000

    Water Pollution Protection
    Personal Services　　　　　　　　　　　$23,000,000
    Supplies and Materials　　　　　　　　　4,500,000
    Capital Outlay　　　　　　　　　　　　20,500,000
       Total Water Pollution Protection　　　　　$ 48,000,000

  Total Environmental Safety　　　　　　　　　　　　　$ 78,000,000

22. Based on the above budget, which is the MOST valid statement?　　　　22._____

    A.　Environmental Safety, Air Pollution Protection, and Water Pollution Protection could
       all be considered program elements.
    B.　The object listings included water pollution protection and capital outlay.
    C.　Examples of the program element listings in the above are personal services and
       supplies and materials.
    D.　Contractual Services and Environmental Safety were the program element listings.

23. Which of the following is NOT an advantage of a program budget over a line-item bud-　　23._____
    get?
    A program budget

    A.　allows us to set up priority lists in deciding what activities we will spend our money
       on
    B.　gives us more control over expenditures than a line-item budget
    C.　is more informative in that we know the broad purposes of spending money
    D.　enables us to see if one program is getting much less money than the others

24. If a manager were trying to explain the fundamental difference between traditional   24.____
    accounting theory and practice and the newer practice of managerial accounting, he
    would be MOST accurate if he said that

    A. traditional accounting practice focused on providing information for persons out-
    side organizations, while managerial accounting focuses on providing information
    for people inside organizations
    B. traditional accounting practice focused on providing information for persons inside
    organizations while managerial accounting focuses on providing information for
    persons outside organizations
    C. managerial accounting is exclusively concerned with historical facts while tradi-
    tional accounting stresses future projections exclusively
    D. traditional accounting practice is more budget-focused than managerial account-
    ing

25. Which of the following formulas is used to determine the number of days required to pro-   25.____
    cess work?

    A. $\dfrac{\text{Employees x Daily Output}}{\text{Volume}}$ = Days to Process Work

    B. $\dfrac{\text{Volume x Daily Output}}{\text{Employees}}$ = Days to Process Work

    C. $\dfrac{\text{Volume}}{\text{Employees x Daily Output}}$ = Days to Process Work

    D. $\dfrac{\text{Employees x Volume}}{\text{Daily Output}}$ = Days to Process Work

KEY (CORRECT ANSWERS)

1.	C	11.	C
2.	C	12.	D
3.	D	13.	A
4.	B	14.	C
5.	D	15.	D
6.	D	16.	C
7.	D	17.	A
8.	A	18.	A
9.	B	19.	B
10.	C	20.	B

21.	D
22.	A
23.	B
24.	A
25.	C

TEST 3

DIRECTIONS: Each question or incomplete statement is followed by several suggested answers or completions. Select the one that BEST answers the question or completes the statement. *PRINT THE LETTER OF THE CORRECT ANSWER IN THE SPACE AT THE RIGHT.*

1. Electronic data processing equipment can produce more information faster than can be generated by any other means.
   In view of this, the MOST important problem faced by management at present is to

   A. keep computers fully occupied
   B. find enough computer personnel
   C. assimilate and properly evaluate the information
   D. obtain funds to establish appropriate information systems

   1.____

2. A well-designed management information system ESSENTIALLY provides each executive and manager the information he needs for

   A. determining computer time requirements
   B. planning and measuring results
   C. drawing a new organization chart
   D. developing a new office layout

   2.____

3. It is generally agreed that management policies should be periodically reappraised and restated in accordance with current conditions.
   Of the following, the approach which would be MOST effective in determining whether a policy should be revised is to

   A. conduct interviews with staff members at all levels in order to ascertain the relationship between the policy and actual practice
   B. make proposed revisions in the policy and apply it to current problems
   C. make up hypothetical situations using both the old policy and a revised version in order to make comparisons
   D. call a meeting of top level staff in order to discuss ways of revising the policy

   3.____

4. Every manager has many occasions to lead a conference or participate in a conference of some sort.
   Of the following statements that pertain to conferences and conference leadership, which is generally considered to be MOST valid?

   A. Since World War II, the trend has been toward fewer shared decisions and more conferences.
   B. The most important part of a conference leader's job is to direct discussion.
   C. In providing opportunities for group interaction, management should avoid consideration of its past management philosophy.
   D. A good administrator cannot lead a good conference if he is a poor public speaker.

   4.____

5. Of the following, it is usually LEAST desirable for a conference leader to

   A. turn the question to the person who asked it
   B. summarize proceedings periodically
   C. make a practice of not repeating questions
   D. ask a question without indicating who is to reply

   5.____

6. The behavioral school of management thought bases its beliefs on certain assumptions. 6.____
   Which of the following is NOT a belief of this school of thought?

   A. People tend to seek and accept responsibility.
   B. Most people can be creative in solving problems.
   C. People prefer security above all else.
   D. Commitment is the most important factor in motivating people.

7. The one of the following objectives which would be LEAST appropriate as a major goal of 7.____
   research in the field of human resources management is to

   A. predict future conditions, events, and manpower needs
   B. evaluate established policies, programs, and practices
   C. evaluate proposed policies, programs, and practices
   D. identify deficient organizational units and apply suitable penalties

8. Of the following general interviewing methods or techniques, the one that is USUALLY 8.____
   considered to be effective in counseling, grievances, and appraisal interviews is the
   _____ interview.

   A. directed   B. non-directed
   C. panel   D. patterned

9. The ESSENTIAL first phase of decision-making is 9.____

   A. finding alternative solutions
   B. making a diagnosis of the problem
   C. selecting the plan to follow
   D. analyzing and comparing alternative solutions

10. Assume that, in a certain organization, a situation has developed in which there is little 10.____
    difference in status or authority between individuals.
    Which of the following would be the MOST likely result with regard to communication in
    this organization?

    A. Both the accuracy and flow of communication will be improved.
    B. Both the accuracy and flow of communication will substantially decrease.
    C. Employees will seek more formal lines of communication.
    D. Neither the flow nor the accuracy of communication will be improved over the
       former hierarchical structure.

11. The main function of many agency administrative offices is *information management.* 11.____
    Information that is received by an administrative officer may be classified as active or
    passive, depending upon whether or not it requires the recipient to take some action.
    Of the following, the item received which is clearly the MOST active information is

    A. an appointment of a new staff member
    B. a payment voucher for a new desk
    C. a press release concerning a past city event
    D. the minutes of a staff meeting

12. Which one of the following sets BEST describes the general order in which to teach an operation to a new employee?   12.____

    A. Prepare, present, tryout, follow-up
    B. Prepare, test, tryout, re-test
    C. Present, test, tryout, follow-up
    D. Test, present, follow-up, re-test

13. Of the following, public employees may be separated from public service   13.____

    A. for the same reasons which are generally acceptable for discharging employees in private industry
    B. only under the most trying circumstances
    C. under procedures that are neither formalized nor subject to review
    D. solely in extreme cases involving offenses of gravest character

14. Of the following, the one LEAST considered to be a communication barrier is   14.____

    A. group feedback   B. charged words
    C. selective perception   D. symbolic meanings

15. Of the following ways for a manager to handle his appointments, the BEST way, according to experts in administration, generally is to   15.____

    A. schedule his own appointments and inform his secretary not to reserve his time without his approval
    B. encourage everyone to make appointments through his secretary and tell her when he makes his own appointments
    C. see no one who has not made a previous appointment
    D. permit anyone to see him without an appointment

16. Assume that a manager decides to examine closely one of five units under his supervision to uncover problems common to all five.
His research technique is MOST closely related to the method called   16.____

    A. experimentation   B. simulation
    C. linear analysis   D. sampling

17. If one views the process of management as a dynamic process, which one of the following functions is NOT a legitimate part of that process?   17.____

    A. Communication   B. Decision-making
    C. Organizational slack   D. Motivation

18. Which of the following would be the BEST statement of a budget-oriented purpose for a government administrator? To   18.____

    A. provide 200 hours of instruction in basic reading for 3500 adult illiterates at a cost of $1 million in the next fiscal year
    B. inform the public of adult educational programs
    C. facilitate the transfer to a city agency of certain functions of a federally-funded program which is being phased out
    D. improve the reading skills of the adult citizens in the city

19. Modern management philosophy and practices are changing to accommodate the expectations and motivations of organization personnel.
Which of the following terms INCORRECTLY describes these newer managerial approaches?

    A. Rational management   B. Participative management
    C. Decentralization   D. Democratic supervision

19._____

20. Management studies support the hypothesis that, in spite of the tendency of employees to censor the information communicated to their supervisor, subordinates are MORE likely to communicate problem-oriented information upward when they have

    A. a long period of service in the organization
    B. a high degree of trust in the supervisor
    C. a high educational level
    D. low status on the organizational ladder

20._____

KEY (CORRECT ANSWERS)

1. C	11. A
2. B	12. A
3. A	13. A
4. B	14. A
5. A	15. B
6. C	16. D
7. D	17. C
8. B	18. A
9. B	19. A
10. D	20. B

EXAMINATION SECTION
TEST 1

DIRECTIONS: Each question or incomplete statement is followed by several suggested answers or completions. Select the one that BEST answers the question or completes the statement. *PRINT THE LETTER OF THE CORRECT ANSWER IN THE SPACE AT THE RIGHT.*

1. In many instances, managers deliberately set up procedures and routines that more than one department or more than one employee is required to complete and verify an entire operation or transaction.
   The MAIN reason for establishing such routines is *generally* to

   A. minimize the chances of gaps and deficiencies in feedback of information to management
   B. expand the individual employee's vision and concern for broader organizational objectives
   C. provide satisfaction of employees' social and egoistic needs through teamwork and horizontal communications
   D. facilitate internal control designed to prevent errors, whether intentional or accidental

   1.____

2. Committees—sometimes referred to as boards, commissions, or task forces—are widely used in government to investigate certain problems or to manage certain agencies.
   Of the following, the MOST serious limitation of the committee approach to management in government is that

   A. it reflects government's inability to delegate authority effectively to individual executives
   B. committee members do not usually have similar backgrounds, experience, and abilities
   C. it promotes horizontal communication at the expense of vertical communication
   D. the spreading out of responsibility to a committee often results in a willingness to settle for weak, compromise solutions

   2.____

3. Of the following, the BEST reason for replacing members of committees on a staggered or partial basis rather than replacing all members simultaneously is that this practice

   A. gives representatives of different interest groups a chance to contribute their ideas
   B. encourages continuity of policy since retained members are familiar with previous actions
   C. prevents interpersonal frictions from building up and hindering the work of the group
   D. improves the quality of the group's recommendations and decisions by stimulating development of new ideas

   3.____

4. Assume that in considering a variety of actions to take to solve a given problem, a manager decides to take no action at all.
   According to generally accepted management practice, such a decision would be

   4.____

A. *proper,* because under normal circumstances, it is better to make no decision
B. *improper,* because inaction would be rightly construed as shunning one's responsibilities
C. *proper,* since this would be a decision which might produce more positive results than the other alternatives
D. *improper,* since such a solution would delay corrective action and exacerbate the problem

5. Some writers in the field of management assume that when a newly promoted manager has been informed by his superior about the subordinates he is to direct and the extent of his authority, that is all that is necessary. However, thereafter, this new manager should realize that, for practical purposes, his authority will be effective ONLY when 5.____

A. he accepts full responsibility for the actions of his subordinates
B. his subordinates are motivated to carry out their assignments
C. it derives from acceptable personal attributes rather than from his official position
D. he exercises it in an authoritarian manner

6. A newly appointed manager is assigned to assist the head of a small developing agency handling innovative programs. Although this manager is a diligent worker, he does not delegate authority to middle- and lower-echelon supervisors. The MOST important reason why it would be desirable to change this attitude toward delegation is because otherwise 6.____

A. he may have to assume more responsibility for the actions of his subordinates than is implied in the authority delegated to him
B. his subordinates will tend to produce innovative solutions on their own
C. the agency will become a decentralized type of organization in which he cannot maintain adequate controls
D. he may not have time to perform other essential tasks

7. All types of organizations and all functions within them are to varying degrees affected today by the need to understand the application of computer systems to management practices.
The one of the following purposes for which such systems would be MOST useful is to 7.____

A. lower the costs of problem-solving by utilizing data that is already in the agency's control system correlated with new data
B. stabilize basic patterns of the organization into long-term structures and relationships
C. give instant solutions to complex problems
D. affect savings in labor costs for office tasks involving non-routine complex problems

8. Compared to individual decision-making, group decision-making is burdened with the DISADVANTAGE of 8.____

A. making snap judgments
B. pressure to examine all relevant elements of the problem
C. greater motivation needed to implement the decision
D. the need to clarify problems for the group participants

84

9. Assume that a manager in an agency, faced with a major administrative problem, has developed a number of alternative solutions to the problem.
Which of the following would be MOST effective in helping the manager make the best decision?

    A. *Experience,* because a manager can distill from the past the fundamental reasons for success or failure since the future generally duplicates the past
    B. *Experimentation,* because it is the method used in scientific inquiry and can be tried out economically in limited areas
    C. *Research analysis,* because it is generally less costly than most other methods and involves the interrelationships among the more critical factors that bear upon the goal sought
    D. *Value forecasting,* because it assigns numerical significance to the values of alternative tangible and intangible choices and indicates the degree of risk involved in each choice

9.____

10. Management information systems operate more effectively for managers than mere data tabulating systems because information systems

    A. eliminate the need for managers to tell information processors what is required
    B. are used primarily for staff rather than line functions
    C. are less expensive to operate than manual methods of data collection
    D. present and utilize data in a meaningful form

10.____

11. Project-type organizations are in widespread use today because they offer a number of advantages.
The MOST important purpose of the project organization is to

    A. secure a higher degree of coordination than could be obtained in a conventional line structure
    B. provide an orderly way of phasing projects in and out of organizations
    C. expedite routine administrative processes
    D. allow for rapid assessment of the status of any given project and its effect on agency productivity

11.____

12. A manager adjusts his plans for future activity by reviewing information about the performance of his subordinates. This is an application of the process of

    A. human factor impact
    B. coordinated response
    C. feedback communication
    D. reaction control

12.____

13. From the viewpoint of the manager in an agency, the one of the following which is the MOST constructive function of a status system or a rank system based on employee performance is that the system

    A. makes possible effective communication, thereby lessening social distances between organizational levels
    B. is helpful to employees of lesser ability because it provides them with an incentive to exceed their capacities
    C. encourages the employees to attain or exceed the goals set for them by the organization
    D. diminishes friction in assignment and work relation-ships of personnel

13.____

14. Some managers ask employees who have been newly hired by their agency and then assigned to their divisions or units such questions as: *What are your personal goals? What do you expect from your job? Why do you want to work for this organization?* For a manager to ask these questions is GENERALLY considered

    14.____

    A. *inadvisable;* these questions should have been asked prior to hiring the employee
    B. *inadvisable;* the answers will arouse subjective prejudices in the manager before he sees what kind of work the employee can do
    C. *advisable;* this approach indicates to the employee that the manager is interested in him as an individual
    D. *advisable;* the manager can judge how much of a disparity exists between the employee's goals and the agency's goals

15. Assume that you have prepared a report to your superior recommending a reorganization of your staff to eliminate two levels of supervision. The total number of employees would remain the same, with the supervisors of the two eliminated levels taking on staff assignments.
In your report, which one of the following should NOT be listed as an expected result of such a reorganization?

    15.____

    A. Fewer breakdowns and distortions in communications to staff
    B. Greater need for training
    C. Broader opportunities for development of employee skills
    D. Fewer employee errors due to exercise of closer supervision and control

16. *Administration* has often been criticized as being unproductive in the sense that it seems far removed from the end products of an organization.
According to modern management thought, this criticism, for the most part, is

    16.____

    A. *invalid,* because administrators make it possible for subordinates to produce goods or services by directing coordinating, and controlling their activities
    B. *valid,* because most subordinates usually do the work required to produce goods and services with only general direction from their immediate superiors
    C. *invalid,* because administrators must see to all of the details associated with the production of services
    D. *valid,* because administrators generally work behind the scenes and are mainly concerned with long-range planning

17. A manager must be able to evaluate the relative importance of his decisions and establish priorities for carrying them out.
Which one of the following factors bearing on the relative importance of making a decision would indicate to a manager that he can delegate that decision to a subordinate or give it low priority? The

    17.____

    A. decision concerns a matter on which strict confiden-tiality must be maintained
    B. community impact of the decision is great
    C. decision can be easily changed
    D. decision commits the agency to a heavy expenditure of funds

18. Suppose that you are responsible for reviewing and submitting to your superior the monthly reports from ten field auditors. Despite your repeated warnings to these audi-tors, most of them hand in their reports close to or after the deadline dates, so that you have no time to return them for revision and find yourself working overtime to make the necessary corrections yourself.
The deadline dates for the auditors' reports and your report cannot be changed.
Of the following, the MOST probable cause for this con-tinuing situation is that

    A. these auditors need retraining in the writing of this type of report
    B. possible disciplinary action as a result of the delay by the auditors has not been impressed upon them
    C. the auditors have had an opportunity to provide you with feedback to explain the reasons for the delays
    D. you, as the manager, have not used disciplinary measures of sufficient severity to change their behavior

18.____

19. Assume that an agency desiring to try out a *management-by-objectives* program has set down the guidelines listed below to implement this activity.
Which one of these guidelines is MOST likely to present obstacles to the success of this type of program?

    A. Specific work objectives should be determined by top management for employees at all levels.
    B. Objectives should be specific, attainable, and preferably measurable as to units, costs, ratios, time, etc.
    C. Standards of performance should be either qualitative or quantitative, preferably quantitative.
    D. There should be recognition and rewards for success-ful achievement of objec-tives.

19.____

20. Of the following, the MOST meaningful way to express productivity where employees work a standard number of hours each day is in terms of the relationship between man-

    A. hours expended and number of work-units needed to produce the final product
    B. days expended and goods and services produced
    C. days and energy expended
    D. days expended and number of workers

20.____

21. Agencies often develop productivity indices for many of their activities.
Of the following, the MOST important use for such indices is *generally* to

    A. measure the agency's output against its own past performance
    B. improve quality standards while letting productivity remain unchanged
    C. compare outputs of the agency with outputs in private industry
    D. determine manpower requirements

21.____

22. The MOST outstanding characteristic of staff authority, such as that of a public relations officer in an agency, as compared with line authority, is *generally* accepted to be

    A. reliance upon personal attributes
    B. direct relationship to the primary objectives of the organization
    C. absence of the right to direct or command
    D. responsibility for attention to technical details

22.____

23. In the traditional organization structure, there are often more barriers to upward communication than to downward communication.
From the viewpoint of a manager whose goal is to overcome obstacles to communication, this situation should be

    23.____

    A. *accepted;* the downward system is the more important since it is highly directive, giving necessary orders, instructions, and procedures
    B. *changed;* the upward system should receive more emphasis than the downward system, which represents stifling bureaucratic authority
    C. *accepted;* it is generally conceded that upward systems supply enough feedback for control purposes necessary to the organization's survival
    D. *changed;* research has generally verified the need for an increase in upward communications to supply more information about employees' ideas, attitudes, and performance

24. A principal difficulty in productivity measurement for local government services is in defining and measuring output, a problem familiar to managers. A measurement that merely looks good, but which may be against the public interest, is another serious problem. Managers should avoid encouraging employees to take actions that lead to such measurements.
In accordance with the foregoing statement, it would be MOST desirable for a manager to develop a productivity measure that

    24.____

    A. correlates the actual productivity measure with impact on benefit to the citizenry
    B. does not allow for a mandated annual increase in productivity
    C. firmly fixes priorities for resource allocations
    D. uses numerical output, by itself, in productivity incentive plans

25. For a manager, the MOST significant finding of the Hawthorne studies and experiments is that an employee's productivity is affected MOST favorably when the

    25.____

    A. importance of tasks is emphasized and there is a logical arrangement of work functions
    B. physical surroundings and work conditions are improved
    C. organization has a good public relations program
    D. employee is given recognition and allowed to participate in decision-making

KEY (CORRECT ANSWERS)

1.	D	11.	A
2.	D	12.	C
3.	B	13.	C
4.	C	14.	A
5.	B	15.	D
6.	D	16.	A
7.	A	17.	C
8.	D	18.	D
9.	C	19.	A
10.	D	20.	B

21.	A
22.	C
23.	D
24.	A
25.	D

TEST 2

1. Which one of the following is generally accepted by managers as the MOST difficult aspect of a training program in staff supervision?

    A. Determining training needs of the staff
    B. Evaluating the effectiveness of the courses
    C. Locating capable instructors to teach the courses
    D. Finding adequate space and scheduling acceptable times for all participants

1.____

2. Assume that, as a manager, you have decided to start a job enrichment program with the purpose of making jobs more varied and interesting in an effort to increase the motivation of a certain group of workers in your division. Which one of the following should generally NOT be part of this program?

    A. Increasing the accountability of these individuals for their own work
    B. Granting additional authority or job freedom to these employees in their job activities
    C. Mandating increased monthly production goals for this group of employees
    D. Giving each of these employees a complete unit of work

2.____

3. Both employer and employee have an important stake in effective preparation for retirement.
According to modern management thinking, the one of the following which is probably the MOST important aspect of a sound pre-retirement program is to

    A. make assignments that utilize the employee's abilities fully
    B. reassign the employee to a less demanding position in the organization for the last year or two he is on the job
    C. provide the employee with financial data and other facts that would be pertinent to his retirement planning
    D. encourage the employee to develop interests and hobbies which are connected with the job

3.____

4. The civil service system generally emphasizes a policy of *promotion-from-within.* Employees in the direct line of promotion in a given occupational group are eligible for promotion to the next higher title in that occupational group.
Which one of the following is LEAST likely to occur as a result of this policy and practice?

    A. Training time will be saved since employees in higher-level positions are already familiar with many agency rules, regulations, and procedures.
    B. The recruitment section will be able to show prospective employees that there are distinct promotional opportunities.
    C. Employees will be provided with a clear-cut picture as to their possible career ladder.
    D. Employees will be encouraged to seek broad-based training and education to enhance their promotability.

4.____

5. From a management point of view, the MAIN drawback of seniority as opposed to merit 5.____
as a basis for granting pay increases to workers is that a pay increase system based on
seniority

    A. is favored by unions
    B. upsets organizational status relationships
    C. may encourage mediocre performance by employees
    D. is more difficult to administer than a merit plan

6. One of the actions that is often taken against employees in the non-uniformed forces 6.____
who are accused of misconduct on the job is suspension without pay.
The MOST justifiable reason for taking such action is to

    A. ease an employee out of the agency
    B. enable an investigation to be conducted into the circumstances of the offense
       where doubt exists about the guilt of the employee
    C. improve the performance of the employee when he returns to the job
    D. punish the employee by imposing a hardship on him

7. A manager has had difficulty in getting good clerical employees to staff a filing section 7.____
under his supervision. To add to his problems, one of his most competent senior clerks
requests a transfer to the accounting division so that he can utilize his new accounting
skill, which he is acquiring by going to college at night. The manager attempts to keep
the senior clerk in his filing section by calling the director of personnel and getting him to
promise not to authorize any transfer. GENERALLY, this manager's action is

    A. *desirable;* he should not help his staff to develop themselves if it means losing
       good people
    B. *undesirable ;* he should recommend that the senior clerk get a raise in the hope of
       preventing him from transferring to another section
    C. *desirable;* it shows that the manager is concerned about the senior clerk's future
       performance
    D. *undesirable;* it is good policy to transfer employees to the type of work they are
       interested in and for which they are acquiring training

8. One of your subordinates, a unit supervisor, comes to you, the division chief, because he 8.____
feels that he is working out of title, and he suggests that his competitive class position
should be reclassified to a higher title.
Which one of the following statements that the subordinate has made is generally
LEAST likely to be a valid support for his suggestion?

    A. The work he is doing conforms to the general statement of duties and responsibili-
       ties as described in the class specification for the next higher title in his occupa-
       tional group.
    B. Most of the typical tasks he performs are listed in the class specification for a title
       with a higher salary range and are not listed for his current title.
    C. His education and experience qualifications far exceed the minimum requirements
       for the position he holds.
    D. His duties and responsibilities have changed recently and are now similar to those
       of his supervisor.

9. Assume that a class specification for a competitive title used exclusively by your agency is outdated, and that no examination for the title has been given since the specification was issued.
Of the following, the MOST appropriate action for your agency to take is to

    A. make the necessary changes and submit the revised class specification to the city civil service commission
    B. write the personnel director to recommend that the class specification be updated, giving the reasons and suggested revisions
    C. prepare a revised class specification and submit it to the office of management and budget for their approval
    D. secure approval of the state civil service commission to update the class specification, and then submit the revised specification to the city civil service commission

9.____

10. Assume that an appropriate eligible list has been established and certified to your agency for a title in which a large number of provisionals are serving in your agency.
In order to obtain permission from the personnel director to retain some of them beyond the usual time limit set by rules (two months) following certification of the list, which one of the following conditions MUST apply?

    A. The positions are sensitive and require investigation of eligibles prior to appointment.
    B. Replacement of all provisionals within two months would impair essential public service.
    C. Employees are required to work rotating shifts, including nights and weekends.
    D. The duties of the positions require unusual physical effort and endurance.

10.____

11. Under the federally-funded Comprehensive Employment and Training Act (CETA), the hiring by the city of non-civil servants for CETA jobs is PROHIBITED when the

    A. applicants are unemployed because of seasonal lay-offs in private industry
    B. applicants do not meet U.S. citizenship and city residence requirements
    C. jobs have minimum requirements of specialized professional or technical training and experience
    D. jobs are comparable to those performed by laid-off civil servants

11.____

12. Assume you are in charge of the duplicating service in your agency. Since employees assigned to this operation lack a sense of accomplishment because the work is highly specialized and repetitive, your superior proposes to enlarge the jobs of these workers and asks you about your reaction to this strategy.
The MOST appropriate response for you to make is that job enlargement would be

    A. *undesirable,* PRIMARILY because it would increase production costs
    B. *undesirable,* PRIMARILY because it would diminish the quality of the output
    C. *desirable,* PRIMARILY because it might make it possible to add an entire level of management to the organizational structure of your agency
    D. *desirable,* PRIMARILY because it might make it possible to decrease the amount of supervision the workers will require

12.____

13. According to civil service law, layoff or demotion must be made in inverse order of seniority among employees permanently serving in the same title and layoff unit. Which one of the following is now the CORRECT formula for computing seniority?
Total continuous service in the

13.____

A. competitive class *only*
B. competitive, non-competitive, or labor class
C. classified or unclassified services
D. competitive, non-competitive, exempt, and labor classes

14. Under which of the following conditions would an appoint-ing officer be permitted to con-sider the sex of a candidate in making an employment decision?
When

    A. the duties of the position require considerable physical effort or strength
    B. the duties of the position are considered inherently dangerous
    C. separate toilet facilities and dressing rooms for the sexes are unavailable and/or cannot be provided in any event
    D. the public has indicated a preference to be served by persons of a specified sex

14.____

15. Assume that an accountant under your supervision signs out to the field to make an agency audit. It is later discovered that, although he had reported himself at work until 5 P.M. that day, he had actually left for home at 3:30 P.M. Although this accountant has worked for the city for ten years and has had an excellent performance record, he is demoted to a lower title in punishment for this breach of duty.
According to generally accepted thinking on personnel management, the disciplinary action taken in this case should be considered

    A. *appropriate;* a lesser penalty might encourage repetition of the offense
    B. *inappropriate;* the correct penalty for such a breach of duty should be dismissal
    C. *appropriate;* the accountant's abilities may be utilized better in the new assignment
    D. *inappropriate;* the impact of a continuing stigma and loss of salary is not commen-surate with the offense committed

15.____

16. Line managers often request more funds for their units than are actually required to attain their current objectives.
Which one of the following is the MOST important reason for such inflated budget requests?
The

    A. expectation that budget examiners will exercise their prerogative of budget cutting
    B. line manager's interest in improving the performance of his unit is thereby indicated to top management
    C. expectation that such requests will make it easier to obtain additional funds in future years
    D. opinion that it makes sense to obtain additional funds and decide later how to use them

16.____

17. Integrating budgeting with program planning and evaluation in a city agency is GENER-ALLY considered to be

    A. *undesirable;* budgeting must focus on the fiscal year at hand, whereas planning must concern itself with developments over a period of years
    B. *desirable;* budgeting facilitates the choice-making process by evaluating the finan-cial implications of agency programs and forcing cost comparisons among them
    C. *undesirable;* accountants and statisticians with the required budgetary skills have little familiarity with the substantive programs that the agency is conducting
    D. *desirable;* such a partnership increases the budgetary skills of planners, thus pro-moting more effective use of public resources

17.____

18. As an aspect of the managerial function, a budget is described BEST as a   18.___

    A. set of qualitative management controls over productivity
    B. tool based on historical accounting reports
    C. type of management plan expressed in quantitative terms
    D. precise estimate of future quantitative and qualitative contingencies

19. Which one of the following is *generally* accepted as the MAJOR immediate advantage of   19.___
installing a system of program budgeting?
It

    A. encourages managers to relate their decisions to the agency's long-range goals
    B. is a replacement for the financial or fiscal budget
    C. decreases the need for managers to make trade-offs in the decision-making pro-
       cess
    D. helps to adjust budget figures to provide for unexpected developments

20. Of the following, the BEST means for assuring necessary responsiveness of a budgetary   20.___
program to changing conditions is by

    A. overestimating budgetary expenditures by 15% and assigning the excess to
       unforeseen problem areas
    B. underestimating budgetary expenditures by at least 20% and setting aside a
       reserve account in the same amount
    C. reviewing and revising the budget at regular intervals so that it retains its character
       as a current document
    D. establishing *budget by exception* policies for each division in the agency

21. According to expert thought in the area of budgeting, participation in the preparation of a   21.___
government agency's budget should GENERALLY involve

    A. only top management
    B. only lower levels of management
    C. all levels of the organization
    D. only a central budget office or bureau

22. Of the following, the MOST useful guide to analysis of budget estimates for the coming   22.___
fiscal year is a com-parison with

    A. appropriations as amended for the current fiscal year
    B. manpower requirements for the previous two years
    C. initial appropriations for the current fiscal year
    D. budget estimates for the preceding five years

23. A manager assigned to analyze the costs and benefits associated with a program which   23.___
the agency head proposes to undertake may encounter certain factors which cannot be
measured in dollar terms.
In such a case, the manager should GENERALLY

    A. ignore the factors which cannot be quantified
    B. evaluate the factors in accordance with their degree of importance to the overall
       agency goals

C. give the factors weight equal to the weight given to measurable costs and benefits
D. assume that non-measurable costs and benefits will balance out against one another

24. If city employees believe that they are receiving adverse treatment in terms of training and disciplinary actions because of their national origin, they may file charges of discrimination with the Federal government's   24.____

A. Human Rights Commission
B. Public Employee Relations Board
C. Equal Employment Opportunity Commission
D. United States Department of Commerce

25. Under existing employment statutes, the city is obligated, as an employer, to take *affirmative action* in certain instances.   25.____
This requirement has been imposed to ensure that

A. employees who are members of minority groups, or women, be given special opportunities for training and promotion even though they are not available to other employees
B. employees or applicants for employment are treated without regard to race, color, religion, sex, or national origin
C. proof exists to show that the city has acted with good intentions in any case where it has disregarded this requirement
D. men and women are treated alike except where State law provides special hour or working conditions for women

—————

KEY (CORRECT ANSWERS)

1.	B	11.	D
2.	C	12.	D
3.	C	13.	D
4.	D	14.	C
5.	C	15.	D
6.	B	16.	A
7.	D	17.	B
8.	C	18.	C
9.	B	19.	A
10.	B	20.	C

21.	C
22.	A
23.	B
24.	C
25.	B

———

EXAMINATION SECTION
TEST 1

DIRECTIONS: Each question or incomplete statement is followed by several suggested answers or completions. Select the one that *BEST* answer the question or completes the statement. *PRINT THE LETTER OF THE CORRECT ANSWER IN THE SPACE AT THE RIGHT.*

1. Although some kinds of instructions are best put in written form, a supervisor can give many instructions verbally.
   In which one of the following situations would verbal instructions be *MOST* suitable?

   A. Furnishing an employee with the details to be checked in doing a certain job
   B. Instructing an employee on the changes necessary to update the office manual used in your unit
   C. Informing a new employee where different kinds of supplies and equipment that he might need are kept
   D. Presenting an assignment to an employee who will be held accountable for following a series of steps

   1._____

2. You may be asked to evaluate the organization structure of your unit.
   Which one of the following questions would you *NOT* expect to take up in an evaluation of this kind?

   A. Is there an employee whose personal problems are interfering with his or her work?
   B. Is there an up-to-date job description for each position in this section?
   C. Are related operations and tasks grouped together and regularly assigned together?
   D. Are responsibilities divided as far as possible, and. is this division clearly understood by all employees?

   2._____

3. In order to distribute and schedule work fairly and efficiently, a supervisor may wish to make a work distribution study. A simple way of getting the information necessary for such a study is to have everyone for one week keep track of each task done and the time spent on each.
   Which one of the following situations showing up in such a study would *most clearly* call for corrective action?

   A. The newest employee takes longer to do most tasks than do experienced employees
   B. One difficult operation takes longer to do than most other operations carried out by the section
   C. A particular employee is very frequently assigned tasks that are not similar and have no relationship to each other
   D. The most highly skilled employee is often assigned the most difficult jobs

   3._____

4. The authority to carry out a job can be delegated to a subordinate, but the supervisor remains responsible for the work of the section as a whole.
   As a supervisor, which of the following rules would be the *BEST* one for you to follow in view of the above statement?

   4._____

A. Avoid assigning important tasks to your subordinates, because you will be blamed if anything goes wrong
B. Be sure each subordinate understands the specific job he has been assigned, and check at intervals to make sure assignments are done properly
C. Assign several people to every important job, so that responsibility will be spread out as much as possible
D. Have an experienced subordinate check all work done by other employees, so that there will be little chance of anything going wrong

5. The human tendency to resist change is often reflected in higher rates of turnover, absenteeism, and errors whenever an important change is made in an organization. Although psychologists do not fully understand the reasons why people resist change, they believe that the resistance stems from a threat to the individual's security, that it is a form of fear of the unknown.
In light of this statement, which one of the following approaches would probably be MOST effective in preparing employees for a change in procedure in their unit?   5.____

A. Avoid letting employees know anything about the change until the last possible moment
B. Sympathize with employees who resent the change and let them know you share their doubts and fears
C. Promise the employees that if the change turns out to be a poor one, you will allow them to suggest a return to the old system
D. Make sure that employees know the reasons for the change and are aware of the benefits that are expected from it

6. Each of the following methods of encouraging employee participation in work planning has been used effectively with different kinds and sizes of employee groups.
Which one of the following methods would be MOST suitable for a group of four technically skilled employees?   6.____

A. Discussions between the supervisor and a representative of the group
B. A suggestion program with semi-annual awards for outstanding suggestions
C. A group discussion summoned whenever a major problem remains unsolved for more than a month
D. Day-to-day exchange of information, opinions and experience

7. Of the following, the MOST important reason why a supervisor is given the authority to tell subordinates what work they should do, how they should do it, and when it should be done is that usually   7.____

A. most people will not work unless there is someone with authority standing over them
B. work is accomplished more effectively if the supervisor plans and coordinates it
C. when division of work is left up to subordinates, there is constant arguing, and very little work is accomplished
D. subordinates are not familiar with the tasks to be performed

8. Fatigue is a factor that affects productivity in all work situations. However, a brief rest period will ordinarily serve to restore a person from fatigue.
According to this statement, which one of the following techniques is most likely to reduce the impact of fatigue on over-all productivity in a unit?   8.____

A. Scheduling several short breaks throughout the day
B. Allowing employees to go home early
C. Extending the lunch period an extra half hour
D. Rotating job assignments every few weeks

9. After giving a new task to an employee, it is a good idea for a supervisor to ask specific questions to make sure that the employee grasps the essentials of the task and sees how it can be carried out. Questions which ask the employee what he thinks or how he feels about an important aspect of the task are particularly effective.
Which one of the following questions is *NOT* the type of question which would be useful in the foregoing situation?

    9.____

A. "Do you feel there will be any trouble meeting the 4:30 deadline?"
B. "How do you feel about the kind of work we do here?"
C. "Do you think that combining those two steps will work all right?"
D. "Can you think of any additional equipment you may need for this process?"

10. Of the following, the *LEAST* important reason for having a *continuous* training program is that

    10.____

A. employees may forget procedures that they have already learned
B. employees may develop short cuts on the job that result in inaccurate work
C. the job continues to change because of new procedures and equipment
D. training is one means of measuring effectiveness and productivity on the job

11. In training a new employee, it is usually advisable to break down the job into meaningful parts and have the new employee master one part before going on to the next.
Of the following, the *BEST* reason for using this technique is to

    11.____

A. let the new employee know the reason for what he is doing and thus encourage him to remain in the unit
B. make the employee aware of the importance of the work and encourage him to work harder
C. show the employee that the work is easy so that he will be encouraged to work faster
D. make it more likely that the employee will experience success and will be encouraged to continue learning the job

12. You may occasionally find a serious error in the work of one of your subordinates.
Of the following, the *BEST* time to discuss such an error with an employee *usually* is

    12.____

A. immediately after the error is found
B. after about two weeks, since you will also be able to point out some good things that the employee has accomplished
C. when you have discovered a pattern of errors on the part of this employee so that he will not be able to dispute your criticism
D. after the error results in a complaint by your own supervisor

13. For very important announcements to the staff, a supervisor should usually use both writ- 13.____
ten and oral communications. For example, when a new procedure is to be introduced,
the supervisor can more easily obtain the group's acceptance by giving his subordinates
a rough draft of the new procedure and calling a meeting of all his subordinates. The
LEAST important benefit of this technique is that it will better enable the supervisor to

    A. explain why the change is necessary
    B. make adjustments in the new procedure to meet valid staff objections
    C. assign someone to carry out the new procedure
    D. answer questions about the new procedure

14. Assume that, while you are interviewing an individual to obtain information, the individual 14.____
pauses in the middle of an answer.
The *BEST* of the following actions for you to take at that time is to

    A. correct any inaccuracies in what he has said
    B. remain silent until he continues
    C. explain your position on the matter being discussed
    D. explain that time is short and that he must complete his story quickly

15. When you are interviewing someone to obtain information, the *BEST* of the following rea- 15.____
sons for you to repeat certain of his exact words is to

    A. assure him that appropriate action will be taken
    B. encourage him to switch to another topic of discussion
    C. assure him that you agree with his point of view
    D. encourage him to elaborate on a point he has made

16. Generally, when writing a letter, the use of precise words and concise sentences is 16.____

    A. *good,* because less time will be required to write the letter
    B. *bad,* because it is most likely that the reader will think the letter is unimportant and
will not respond favorably
    C. *good,* because it is likely that your desired meaning will be conveyed to the reader
    D. *bad,* because your letter will be too brief to provide adequate information

17. In which of the following cases would it be *MOST* desirable to have *two* cards for one 17.____
individual in a *single* alphabetic file? The individual has

    A. a hyphenated surname   B. two middle names
    C. a first name with an unusual spelling
    D. a compound first name

18. Of the following, it is *MOST* appropriate to use a form letter when it is necessary to 18.____
answer many

    A. requests or inquiries from a single individual
    B. follow-up letters from individuals requesting additional information
    C. requests or inquiries about a single subject
    D. complaints from individuals that they have been unable to obtain various types of
information

19. Assume that you are asked to make up a budget for your section for the coming year, and you are told that the most important function of the budget is its "control function."
Of the following, "control" in this context implies, *most nearly,* that

    A. you will probably be asked to justify expenditures in any category when it looks as though these expenditures are departing greatly from the amount budgeted
    B. your section will probably not be allowed to spend more than the budgeted amount in any given category, although it is always permissible to spend less
    C. your section will be required to spend the exact amount budgeted in every category
    D. the budget will be filed in the Office of the Comptroller so that when the year is over the actual expenditures can be compared with the amounts in the budget

19.____

20. In writing a report, the practice of taking up the *least* important points *first* and the *most* important points *last* is a

    A. *good technique* since the final points made in a report will make the greatest impression on the reader
    B. *good technique* since the material is presented in a more logical manner and will lead directly to the conclusions
    C. *poor technique* since the reader's time is wasted by having to review irrelevant information before finishing the report
    D. *poor technique* since it may cause the reader to lose interest in the report and arrive at incorrect conclusions about the report

20.____

21. Typically, when the technique of "supervision by results" is practiced, higher management sets down, either implicitly or explicitly, certain performance standards or goals that the subordinate is expected to meet. So long as these standards are met, management interferes very little.
The *most likely* result of the use of this technique is that it will

    A. lead to ambiguity in terms of goals
    B. be successful only to the extent that close direct supervision is practiced
    C. make it possible to evaluate both employee and supervisory effectiveness
    D. allow for complete dependence on the subordinate's part

21.____

22. When making written evaluations and reviews of the performance of subordinates, it is *usually ADVISABLE* to

    A. avoid informing the employee of the evaluation if it is critical because it may create hard feelings
    B. avoid informing the employee of the evaluation whether critical or favorable because it is tension-producing
    C. to permit the employee to see the evaluation but not to discuss it with him because the supervisor cannot be certain where the discussion might lead
    D. to discuss the evaluation openly with the employee because it helps the employee understand what is expected of him

22.____

23. There are a number of well-known and respected human relations principles that successful supervisors have been using for years in building good relationships with their employees. Which of the following does NOT illustrate such a principle?

23.____

A. Give clear and complete instructions
B. Let each person know how he is getting along
C. Keep an open-door policy
D. Make all relationships personal ones

24. Assume that it is necessary for you to give an unpleasant assignment to one of your sub-   24.____
ordinates. You expect this employee to raise some objections to this assignment.
The *most appropriate of* the following actions for you to take *FIRST* is to issue the
assignment

    A. *orally,* with the further statement that you will not listen to any complaints
    B. *in writing,* to forestall any complaints by the employee
    C. *orally,* permitting the employee to express his feelings
    D. *in writing,* with a note that any comments should be submitted in writing

25. Suppose you have just announced at a staff meeting with your subordinates that a radi-   25.____
cal reorganization of work will take place next week. Your subordinates at the meeting
appear to be excited, tense, and worried.
Of the following, the *BEST* action for you to take at that time is to

    A. schedule private conferences with each subordinate to obtain his reaction to the
      meeting
    B. close the meeting and tell your subordinates to return immediately to their work
      assignments
    C. give your subordinates some time to ask questions and discuss your announce-
      ment
    D. insist that your subordinates do not discuss your announcement among them-
      selves or with other members of the agency

KEY (CORRECT ANSWERS)

1.	C		11.	D
2.	A		12.	A
3.	C		13.	C
4.	B		14.	B
5.	D		15.	D
6.	D		16.	C
7.	B		17.	A
8.	A		18.	C
9.	B		19.	A
10.	D		20.	D

21.	C
22.	D
23.	D
24.	C
25.	C

TEST 2

DIRECTIONS: Each question or incomplete statement is followed by several suggested answers or completions. Select the one that *BEST* answer the question or completes the statement. *PRINT THE LETTER OF THE CORRECT ANSWER IN THE SPACE AT THE RIGHT.*

1. Of the following, the *BEST* way for a supervisor to increase employees' interest in their work is to   1.____

    A. allow them to make as many decisions as possible
    B. demonstrate to them that he is as technically competent as they
    C. give each employee a difficult assignment
    D. promptly convey to them instructions from higher manage-ment

2. The *one* of the following which is *LEAST* important in maintaining a high level of productivity on the part of employees is the   2.____

    A. provision of optimum physical working conditions for employees
    B. strength of employees' aspirations for promotion
    C. anticipated satisfactions which employees hope to derive from their work
    D. employees' interest in their jobs

3. Of the following, the *MAJOR* advantage of group problem-solving, as compared to individual problem-solving, is that groups will *more readily*   3.____

    A. abide by their own decisions
    B. agree with agency management
    C. devise new policies and procedures
    D. reach conclusions sooner

4. The group problem-solving conference is a useful supervisory method for getting people to reach solutions to problems.
Of the following the *reason* that groups usually reach more realistic solutions than do individuals is that   4.____

    A. individuals, as a rule, take longer than do groups in reaching decisions and are therefore more likely to make an error
    B. bringing people together to let them confer impresses participants with the seriousness of problems
    C. groups are generally more concerned with the future in evaluating organizational problems
    D. the erroneous opinions of group members tend to be corrected by the other members

5. A competent supervisor should be able to distinguish between human and technical problems.
Of the following, the *MAJOR* difference between such problems is that serious human problems, in comparison to ordinary technical problems,   5.____

    A. are remedied more quickly
    B. involve a lesser need for diagnosis
    C. are more difficult to define
    D. become known through indications which are usually the actual problem

6. Of the following, the *BEST* justification for a public agency establishing an alcoholism program for its employees is that

    A.   alcoholism has traditionally been looked upon with a certain amused tolerance by management and thereby ignored as a serious illness
    B.   employees with drinking problems have twice as many on-the-job accidents, especially during the early years of the problem
    C.   excessive use of alcohol is associated with personality instability hindering informal social relationships among peers and subordinates
    D.   the agency's public reputation will suffer despite an employee's drinking problem being a personal matter of little public concern

6.____

7. Assume you are a manager and you find a group of maintenance employees assigned to your project drinking and playing cards for money in an incinerator room after their regular working hours.
The one of the following actions it would be *BEST* for you to take is to

    A.   suspend all employees immediately if there is no question in your mind as to the validity of the charges
    B.   review the personnel records of those involved with the supervisor and make a joint decision on which employees should sustain penalties of loss of annual leave or fines
    C.   ask the supervisor to interview each violator and submit written reports to you and thereafter consult with the supervisor about disciplinary actions
    D.   deduct three days of annual leave from each employee involved if he pleads guilty in lieu of facing more serious charges

7.____

8. Assume that as a manager you must discipline a subordinate, but all of the pertinent facts necessary for a full determination of the appropriate disciplinary action to take are not yet available. However, you fear that a delay in disciplinary action may damage the morale of other employees.
The one of the following which is *MOST* appropriate for you to do in this matter is to

    A.   take immediate disciplinary action as if all the pertinent facts were available
    B.   wait until all the pertinent facts are available before reaching a decision
    C.   inform the subordinate that you know he is guilty, issue a stern warning, and then let him wait for your further act ion
    D.   reduce the severity of the discipline appropriate for the violation

8.____

9. There are two standard dismissal procedures utilized by most public agencies. The first is the "open back door" policy, in which the decision of a supervisor in discharging an employee for reasons of inefficiency cannot be cancelled by the central personnel agency. The second is the "closed back door" policy, in which the central personnel agency can order the supervisor to restore the discharged employee to his position.
Of the following, the *major DISADVANTAGE* of the "closed back door" policy as opposed to the "open back door" policy is that central personnel agencies are

    A.   likely to approve the dismissal of employees when there is inadequate justification
    B.   likely to revoke dismissal actions out of sympathy for employees
    C.   less qualified than employing agencies to evaluate the efficiency of employees
    D.   easily influenced by political, religious, and racial factors

9.____

10. The one of the following for which a formal grievance-handling system is *LEAST* useful is in   10.____

    A. reducing the frequency of employee complaints
    B. diminishing the likelihood of arbitrary action by supervisors
    C. providing an outlet for employee frustrations
    D. bringing employee problems to the attention of higher management

11. The one of the following managers whose leadership style involves the *GREATEST* delegation of authority to subordinates is the one who presents to subordinates   11.____

    A. his ideas and invites questions
    B. his decision and persuades them to accept it
    C. the problem, gets their suggestions, and makes his decision
    D. a tentative decision which is subject to change

12. Which of the following is *most likely* to cause employee productivity standards to be set too high?   12.____

    A. Standards of productivity are set by first-line supervisors rather than by higher-level managers.
    B. Employees' opinions about productivity standards are sought through written questionnaires.
    C. Initial studies concerning productivity are conducted by staff specialists.
    D. Ideal work conditions assumed in the productivity standards are lacking in actual operations.

13. The one of the following which states the *MAIN* value of an organization chart for a manager is that such charts show the   13.____

    A. lines of formal authority
    B. manner in which duties are performed by each employee
    C. flow of work among employees on the same level
    D. specific responsibilities of each position

14. Which of the following *BEST* names the usual role of a line unit with regard to the organization's programs?   14.____

    A. Seeking publicity   B. Developing
    C. Carrying out   D. Evaluating

15. Critics of promotion *from within* a public agency argue for hiring *from outside* the agency because they believe that promotion from within leads to   15.____

    A. resentment and consequent weakened morale on the part of those not promoted
    B. the perpetuation of outdated practices and policies
    C. a more complex hiring procedure than hiring from outside the agency
    D. problems of objectively appraising someone already in the organization

16. The one of the following management functions which *usually* can be handled *MOST* effectively by a committee is the   16.____

    A. settlement of interdepartmental disputes
    B. planning of routine work schedules
    C. dissemination of information
    D. assignment of personnel

17. Assume that you are serving on a committee which is considering proposals in order to recommend a new maintenance policy. After eliminating a number of proposals by unanimous consent, the committee is deadlocked on three proposals.
The one of the following which is the *BEST* way for the committee to reach agreement on a proposal they could recommend is to

    A. consider and vote on each proposal separately by secret ballot
    B. examine and discuss the three proposals until the proponents of two of them are persuaded they are wrong
    C. reach a synthesis which incorporates the significant features of each proposal
    D. discuss the three proposals until the proponents of each one concede those aspects of the proposals about which there is disagreement

17._____

18. A commonly used training and development method for professional staff is the case method, which utilizes the description of a situation, real or simulated, to provide a common base for analysis, discussion, and problem-solving.
Of the following, the *MOST* appropriate time to use the case method is when professional staff needs

    A. insight into their personality problems
    B. practice in applying management concepts to their own problems
    C. practical experience in the assignment of delegated responsibilities
    D. to know how to function in many different capacities

18._____

19. The incident process is a training and development method in which trainees are given a very brief statement of an event or of a situation presenting a job incident or an employee problem of special significance.
Of the following, it is *MOST* appropriate to use the incident process when

    A. trainees need to learn to review and analyze facts before solving a problem
    B. there are a large number of trainees who require the same information
    C. there are too many trainees to carry on effective discussion
    D. trainees are not aware of the effect of their behavior on others

19._____

20. The one of the following types of information about which a new clerical employee is usually *LEAST* concerned during the orientation process is

    A. his specific job duties   B. where he will work
    C. his organization's history   D. who his associates will be

20._____

21. The one of the following which is the *MOST* important limitation on the degree to which work should be broken down into specialized tasks is the point at which

    A. there ceases to be sufficient work of a specialized nature to occupy employees
    B. training costs equal the half-yearly savings derived from further specialization
    C. supervision of employees performing specialized tasks becomes more technical than supervision of general employees
    D. it becomes more difficult to replace the specialist than to replace the generalist who performs a complex set of functions

21._____

22. When a supervisor is asked for his opinion of the suitability for promotion of a subordi-   22.____
nate, the supervisor is actually being asked to predict the subordinate's future behavior in
a new role.
Such a prediction is *most likely* to be accurate if the

    A. higher position is similar to the subordinate's current one
    B. higher position requires intangible personal qualities
    C. new position requires a high intellectual level of performance
    D. supervisor has had little personal association with the subordinate away from the
       job

23. In one form of the non-directive evaluation interview the supervisor communicates his   23.____
evaluation to the employee and then listens to the employee's response without making
further suggestions.
The one of the following which is the *PRINCIPAL* danger of this method of evaluation is
that the employee is most likely to

    A. develop an indifferent attitude towards the supervisor
    B. fail to discover ways of improving his performance
    C. become resistant to change in the organization's structure
    D. place the blame for his shortcomings on his co-workers

24. In establishing rules for his subordinates, a superior should be *PRIMARILY* concerned   24.____
with

    A. creating sufficient flexibility to allow for exceptions
    B. making employees aware of the reasons for the rules and the penalties for infrac-
       tions
    C. establishing the strength of his own position in relation to his subordinates
    D. having his subordinates know that such rules will be imposed in a personal manner

25. The practice of conducting staff training sessions on a periodic basis is *generally* consid-   25.____
ered

    A. *poor;* it takes employees away from their work assignments
    B. *poor;* all staff training should be done on an individual basis
    C. *good;* it permits the regular introduction of new methods and techniques
    D. *good;* it ensures a high employee productivity rate

KEY (CORRECT ANSWERS)

1.	A		11.	C
2.	A		12.	D
3.	A		13.	A
4.	D		14.	C
5.	C		15.	B
6.	B		16.	A
7.	C		17.	C
8.	B		18.	B
9.	C		19.	A
10.	A		20.	C

21.	A
22.	A
23.	B
24.	B
25.	C

PRINCIPLES AND PRACTICES OF ADMINISTRATION, SUPERVISION & MANAGEMENT

TABLE OF CONTENTS

PRINCIPLES AND PRACTICES OF ADMINISTRATION, SUPERVISION & MANAGEMENT

Most people are inclined to think of administration as something that only a few persons are responsible for in a large organization. Perhaps this is true if you are thinking of Administration with a capital *A*, but administration with a lower case a is a responsibility of supervisors at all levels each working day.

All of us feel we are pretty good supervisors and that we do a good job of administering the workings of our agency. By and large, this is true, but every so often it is good to check up on ourselves. Checklists appear from time to time in various publications which psychologists say, tell whether or not a person will make a good wife, husband, doctor, lawyer, or supervisor.

The following questions are an excellent checklist to test yourself as a supervisor and administrator.

Remember, Administration gives direction and points the way but administration carries the ideas to fruition. Each is dependent on the other for its success. Remember, too, that no unit is too small for these departmental functions to be carried out. These statements apply equally as well to the Chief Librarian as to the Department Head with but one or two persons to supervise.

GENERAL ADMINISTRATION - General Responsibilities of Supervisors

1. Have I prepared written statements of functions, activities, and duties for my organizational unit?

2. Have I prepared procedural guides for operating activities?

3. Have I established clearly in writing, lines of authority and responsibility for my organizational unit?

4. Do I make recommendations for improvements in organization, policies, administrative and operating routines and procedures, including simplification of work and elimination of non-essential operations?

5. Have I designated and trained an understudy to function in my absence?

6. Do I supervise and train personnel within the unit to effectively perform their assignments?

7. Do I assign personnel and distribute work on such a basis as to carry out the organizational unit's assignment or mission in the most effective and efficient manner?

8. Have I established administrative controls by:

    a. Fixing responsibility and accountability on all supervisors under my direction for the proper performance of their functions and duties.

b. Preparing and submitting periodic work load and progress reports covering the operations of the unit to my immediate superior.

c. Analysis and evaluation of such reports received from subordinate units.

d. Submission of significant developments and problems arising within the organizational unit to my immediate superior.

e. Conducting conferences, inspections, etc., as to the status and efficiency of unit operations.

9. Do I maintain an adequate and competent working force?

10. Have I fostered good employee-department relations, seeing that established rules, regulations, and instructions are being carried out properly?

11. Do I collaborate and consult with other organizational units performing related functions to insure harmonious and efficient working relationships?

12. Do I maintain liaison through prescribed channels with city departments and other governmental agencies concerned with the activities of the unit?

13. Do I maintain contact with and keep abreast of the latest developments and techniques of administration (professional societies, groups, periodicals, etc.) as to their applicability to the activities of the unit?

14. Do I communicate with superiors and subordinates through prescribed organizational channels?

15. Do I notify superiors and subordinates in instances where bypassing is necessary as soon thereafter as practicable?

16. Do I keep my superior informed of significant developments and problems?

SEVEN BASIC FUNCTIONS OF THE SUPERVISOR

1. <u>PLANNING</u>
    This means working out goals and means to obtain goals. <u>What</u> needs to be done, <u>who</u> will do it, <u>how</u>, <u>when</u>, and <u>where</u> it is to be done.

    <u>SEVEN STEPS IN PLANNING</u>

    1. Define job or problem clearly.
    2. Consider priority of job.
    3. Consider time-limit - starting and completing.
    4. Consider minimum distraction to, or interference with, other activities.
    5. Consider and provide for contingencies - possible emergencies.
    6. Break job down into components.
    7. Consider the 5 W's and H:

WHY	...	is it necessary to do the job? (Is the purpose clearly defined?)
WHAT	...	needs to be done to accomplish the defined purpose?
	...	is needed to do the job? (money, materials, etc.)
WHO	...	is needed to do the job?
	...	will have responsibilities?
WHERE	...	is the work to be done?
WHEN	...	is the job to begin and end? (schedules, etc.)
HOW	...	is the job to be done? (methods, controls, records, etc.)

2. ORGANIZING

This means dividing up the work, establishing clear lines of responsibility and authority and coordinating efforts to get the job done.

3. STAFFING

The whole personnel function of bringing in and training staff, getting the right man and fitting him to the right job - the job to which he is best suited.

In the normal situation, the supervisor's responsibility regarding staffing normally includes providing accurate job descriptions, that is, duties of the jobs, requirements, education and experience, skills, physical, etc.; assigning the work for maximum use of skills; and proper utilization of the probationary period to weed out unsatisfactory employees.

4. DIRECTING

Providing the necessary leadership to the group supervised. Important work gets done to the supervisor's satisfaction.

5. COORDINATING

The all-important duty of inter-relating the various parts of the work.

The supervisor is also responsible for controlling the coordinated activities. This means measuring performance according to a time schedule and setting quotas to see that the goals previously set are being reached. Reports from workers should be analyzed, evaluated, and made part of all future plans.

6. REPORTING

This means proper and effective communication to your superiors, subordinates, and your peers (in definition of the job of the supervisor). Reports should be read and information contained therein should be used not be filed away and forgotten. Reports should be written in such a way that the desired action recommended by the report is forthcoming.

7. BUDGETING

This means controlling current costs and forecasting future costs. This forecast is based on past experience, future plans and programs, as well as current costs.

You will note that these seven functions can fall under three topics:

Planning	)	
Organizing	)	Make a Plan
Staffing	)	
Directing	)	Get things done
Controlling	)	

Reporting   )
Budgeting   )   Watch it work

PLANNING TO MEET MANAGEMENT GOALS

I. <u>WHAT IS PLANNING?</u>
   A. Thinking a job through before new work is done to determine the best way to do it
   B. A method of doing something
   C. Ways and means for achieving set goals
   D. A means of enabling a supervisor to deliver with a minimum of effort, all details involved in coordinating his work

II. <u>WHO SHOULD MAKE PLANS?</u>
   Everybody!
   All levels of supervision must plan work. (Top management, heads of divisions or bureaus, first line supervisors, and individual employees.) The higher the level, the more planning required.

III. <u>WHAT ARE THE RESULTS OF POOR PLANNING?</u>
   A. Failure to meet deadline
   B. Low employee morale
   C. Lack of job coordination
   D. Overtime is frequently necessary
   E. Excessive cost, waste of material and manhours

IV. <u>PRINCIPLES OF PLANNING</u>
   A. Getting a clear picture of your objectives. What exactly are you trying to accomplish?
   B. Plan the whole job, then the parts, in proper sequence.
   C. Delegate the planning of details to those responsible for executing them.
   D. Make your plan flexible.
   E. Coordinate your plan with the plans of others so that the work may be processed with a minimum of delay.
   F. Sell your plan before you execute it.
   G. Sell your plan to your superior, subordinate, in order to gain maximum participation and coordination.
   H. Your plan should take precedence. Use knowledge and skills that others have brought to a similar job.
   I. Your plan should take account of future contingencies; allow for future expansion.
   J. Plans should include minor details. Leave nothing to chance that can be anticipated.
   K. Your plan should be simple and provide standards and controls. Establish quality and quantity standards and set a standard method of doing the job. The controls will indicate whether the job is proceeding according to plan.
   L. Consider possible bottlenecks, breakdowns, or other difficulties that are likely to arise.

V. Q. WHAT ARE THE *YARDSTICKS* BY WHICH PLANNING SHOULD BE MEASURED?
   A. Any plan should:
      - Clearly state a definite course of action to be followed and goal to be achieved, with consideration for emergencies.
      - Be realistic and practical.

- State what's to be done, when it's to be done, where, how, and by whom.
- Establish the most efficient sequence of operating steps so that more is accomplished in less time, with the least effort, and with the best quality results.
- Assure meeting deliveries without delays.
- Establish the standard by which performance is to be judged.

Q. WHAT KINDS OF PLANS DOES EFFECTIVE SUPERVISION REQUIRE?
A. Plans should cover such factors as:
- Manpower - right number of properly trained employees on the job.
- Materials - adequate supply of the right materials and supplies.
- Machines - full utilization of machines and equipment, with proper maintenance.
- Methods - most efficient handling of operations.
- Deliveries - making deliveries on time.
- Tools - sufficient well-conditioned tools
- Layout - most effective use of space.
- Reports - maintaining proper records and reports.
- Supervision - planning work for employees and organizing supervisor's own time.

I. MANAGEMENT

Question: *What do we mean by management?*

Answer: *Getting work done through others.*

Management could also be defined as planning, directing, and controlling the operations of a bureau or division so that all factors will function properly and all persons cooperate efficiently for a common objective.

II. MANAGEMENT PRINCIPLES

1. There should be a hierarchy - wherein authority and responsibility run upward and downward through several levels - with a broad base at the bottom and a single head at the top.

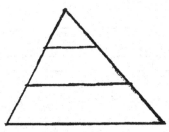

2. Each and every unit or person in the organization should be answerable ultimately to the manager at the apex. In other words, *The buck stops here!*

3. Every necessary function involved in the bureau's objectives is assigned to a unit in that bureau.

4. Responsibilities assigned to a unit are specifically clear-cut and understood.

5. Consistent methods of organizational structure should be applied at each level of the organization.

6. Each member of the bureau from top to bottom knows:
   > to whom he reports
   > who reports to him.

7. No member of one bureau reports to more than one supervisor.
   > No dual functions

8. Responsibility for a function is matched by authority necessary to perform that function.
   > Weight of authority

9. Individuals or units reporting to a supervisor do not exceed the number which can be feasibly and effectively coordinated and directed.
   > Concept of *span of control*

10. Channels of command (management) are not violated by staff units, although there should be staff services to facilitate and coordinate management functions.

11. Authority and responsibility should be decentralized to units and individuals who are responsible for the actual performance of operations.
    > Welfare - down to Welfare Centers
    > Hospitals - down to local hospitals

12. Management should exercise control through attention to policy problems of exceptional importance, rather than through review of routine actions of subordinates.

13. Organizations should never be permitted to grow so elaborate as to hinder work accomplishments.
    > *Empire building*

II. ORGANIZATION STRUCTURE
Types of Organizations.
The purest form is a leader and a few followers, such as:

```
                          [ Supervisor ]
  _____|_____
  |               |                |               |
[ Worker ]    [ Worker ]      [ Worker ]      [ Worker ]
```

(Refer to organization chart) from supervisor to workers.

The line of authority is direct, The workers know exactly where they stand in relation to their boss, to whom they report for instructions and direction.

Unfortunately, in our present complex society, few organizations are similar to this example of a pure line organization. In this era of specialization, other people are often needed in the simplest of organizations. These specialists are known as staff. The sole purpose for their existence (staff) is to assist, advise, suggest, help or counsel line organizations. Staff has no authority to direct line people - nor do they give them direct instructions.

```
                    ┌──────────────┐
                    │  SUPERVISOR  │
                    └──────┬───────┘
        ┌────────────┬─────┴──────┬────────────┐
  ┌───────────┐ ┌───────────┐ ┌───────────┐ ┌────────┐
  │ Personnel │ │Accounting │ │Inspection │ │  Legal │
  └───────────┘ └───────────┘ └───────────┘ └────────┘
  ┌───────────┐ ┌───────────┐ ┌───────────┐ ┌────────┐
  │  Worker   │ │  Worker   │ │  Worker   │ │ Worker │
  └───────────┘ └───────────┘ └───────────┘ └────────┘
```

Line Functions	Staff Functions
1. Directs	1. Advises
2. Orders	2. Persuades and sells
3. Responsibility for carrying out activities from beginning to end	3. Staff studies, reports, recommends but does not carry out
4. Follows chain of command	4. May advise across department lines
5. Is identified with what it does	5. May find its ideas identified with others
6. Decides when and how to use staff advice	6. Has to persuade line to want its advice
7. Line executes	7. Staff - Conducts studies and research. Provides advice and instructions in technical matters. Serves as technical specialist to render specific services

Types and Functions of Organization Charts.

An organization chart is a picture of the arrangement and inter-relationship of the subdivisions of an organization.

1. Types of Charts:
   a. Structural - basic relationships only
   b. Functional - includes functions or duties
   c. Personnel - positions, salaries, status, etc.
   d. Process Chart - work performed
   e. Gantt Chart - actual performance against planned
   f. Flow Chart - flow and distribution of work

2. Functions of Charts:
   a. Assist in management planning and control
   b. Indicate duplication of functions
   c. Indicate incorrect stressing of functions
   d. Indicate neglect of important functions
   e. Correct unclear authority
   f. Establish proper span of control

3. Limitations of Charts:
   a. Seldom maintained on current basis

b. Chart is oversimplified
c. Human factors cannot adequately be charted

4. Organization Charts should be:
   a. Simple
   b. Symmetrical
   c. Indicate authority
   d. Line and staff relationship differentiated
   e. Chart should be dated and bear signature of approving officer
   f. Chart should be displayed, not hidden

ORGANIZATION

There are four basic principles of organization:

1. Unity of command
2. Span of control
3. Uniformity of assignment
4. Assignment of responsibility and delegation of authority

Unity of Command

Unity of command means that each person in the organization should receive orders from one, and only one, supervisor. When a person has to take orders from two or more people, (a) the orders may be in conflict and the employee is upset because he does not know which he should obey, or, (b) different orders may reach him at the same time and he does not know which he should carry out first.

Equally as bad as having two bosses is the situation where the supervisor is by-passed. Let us suppose you are a supervisor whose boss by-passes you (deals directly with people reporting to you). To the worker, it is the same as having two bosses; but to you, the supervisor, it is equally serious. By-passing on the part of your boss will undermine your authority, and the people under you will begin looking to your boss for decisions and even for routine orders.

You can prevent by-passing by telling the people you supervise that if anyone tries to give them orders, they should direct that person to you.

Span of Control

Span of control on a given level involves:

a. The number of people being supervised
b. The distance
c. The time involved in supervising the people. (One supervisor cannot supervise too many workers effectively.)

Span of control means that a supervisor has the right number (not too many and not too few) of subordinates that he can supervise well.

Uniformity of Assignment

In assigning work, you as the supervisor should assign to each person jobs that are similar in nature. An employee who is assigned too many different types of jobs will waste time in going from one kind of work to another. It takes time for him to get to top production in one kind of task and, before he does so, he has to start on another.

When you assign work to people, remember that:

a. Job duties should be definite. Make it clear from the beginning <u>what</u> they are to do, <u>how</u> they are to do it, and <u>why</u> they are to do it. Let them know how much they are expected to do and how well they are expected to do it.

b. Check your assignments to be certain that there are no workers with too many unrelated duties, and that no two people have been given overlapping responsibilities. Your aim should be to have every task assigned to a specific person with the work fairly distributed and with each person doing his part.

<u>Assignment of Responsibility and Delegation of Authority</u>
A supervisor cannot delegate his final responsibility for the work of his department. The experienced supervisor knows that he gets his work done through people. He can't do it all himself. So he must assign the work and the responsibility for the work to his employees. Then they must be given the authority to carry out their responsibilities.

By assigning responsibility and delegating authority to carry out the responsibility, the supervisor builds in his workers initiative, resourcefulness, enthusiasm, and interest in their work. He is treating them as responsible adults. They can find satisfaction in their work, and they will respect the supervisor and be loyal to the supervisor.

PRINCIPLES OF ORGANIZATION

1. <u>Definition</u>
    Organization is the method of dividing up the work to provide the best channels for coordinated effort to get the agency's mission accomplished.

2. <u>Purpose of Organization</u>
    a. To enable each employee within the organization to clearly know his responsibilities and relationships to his fellow employees and to organizational units.
    b. To avoid conflicts of authority and overlapping of jurisdiction.
    c. To ensure teamwork.

3. <u>Basic Considerations in Organizational Planning</u>
    a. The basic plans and objectives of the agency should be determined, and the organizational structure should be adapted to carry out effectively such plans and objectives.
    b. The organization should be built around the major functions of the agency and not individuals or groups of individuals.
    c. The organization should be sufficiently flexible to meet new and changing conditions which may be brought about from within or outside the department.
    d. The organizational structure should be as simple as possible and the number of organizational units kept at a minimum.
    e. The number of levels of authority should be kept at a minimum. Each additional management level lengthens the chain of authority and responsibility and increases the time for instructions to be distributed to operating levels and for decisions to be obtained from higher authority.

f. The form of organization should permit each executive to exercise maximum initiative within the limits of delegated authority.

4. Bases for Organization
   a. Purpose (Examples: education, police, sanitation)
   b. Process (Examples: accounting, legal, purchasing)
   c. Clientele (Examples: welfare, parks, veteran)
   d. Geographic (Examples: borough offices, precincts, libraries)

5. Assignments of Functions
   a. Every function of the agency should be assigned to a specific organizational unit. Under normal circumstances, no single function should be assigned to more than one organizational unit.
   b. There should be no overlapping, duplication, or conflict between organizational elements.
   c. Line functions should be separated from staff functions, and proper emphasis should be placed on staff activities.
   d. Functions which are closely related or similar should normally be assigned to a single organizational unit.
   e. Functions should be properly distributed to promote balance, and to avoid overemphasis of less important functions and underemphasis of more essential functions.

6. Delegation of Authority and Responsibility
   a. Responsibilities assigned to a specific individual or organizational unit should carry corresponding authority, and all statements of authority or limitations thereof should be as specific as possible.
   b. Authority and responsibility for action should be decentralized to organizational units and individuals responsible for actual performance to the greatest extent possible, without relaxing necessary control over policy or the standardization of procedures. Delegation of authority will be consistent with decentralization of responsibility but such delegation will not divest an executive in higher authority of his overall responsibility.
   c. The heads of organizational units should concern themselves with important matters and should delegate to the maximum extent details and routines performed in the ordinary course of business.
   d. All responsibilities, authorities, and relationships should be stated in simple language to avoid misinterpretation.
   e. Each individual or organizational unit charged with a specific responsibility will be held responsible for results.

7. Employee Relationships
   a. The employees reporting to one executive should not exceed the number which can be effectively directed and coordinated. The number will depend largely upon the scope and extent of the responsibilities of the subordinates.
   b. No person should report to more than one supervisor. Every supervisor should know who reports to him, and every employee should know to whom he reports. Channels of authority and responsibility should not be violated by staff units.
   c. Relationships between organizational units within the agency and with outside organizations and associations should be clearly stated and thoroughly understood to avoid misunderstanding.

DELEGATING

1. <u>What is Delegating</u>?
    Delegating is assigning a job to an employee, giving him the authority to get that job done, and giving him the responsibility for seeing to it that the job is done.

    a. <u>What to Delegate</u>
        (1)   Routine details
        (2)   Jobs which may be necessary and take a lot of time, but do not have to be done by the supervisor personally (preparing reports, attending meetings, etc.)
        (3)   Routine decision-making (making decisions which do not require the supervisor's personal attention)

    b. <u>What Not to Delegate</u>
        (1)   Job details which are *executive functions* (setting goals, organizing employees into a good team, analyzing results so as to plan for the future)
        (2)   Disciplinary power (handling grievances, preparing service ratings, reprimands, etc.)
        (3)   Decision-making which involves large numbers of employees or other bureaus and departments
        (4)   Final and complete responsibility for the job done by the unit being supervised

    c. <u>Why Delegate</u>?
        (1)   To strengthen the organization by developing a greater number of skilled employees
        (2)   To improve the employee's performance by giving him the chance to learn more about the job, handle some responsibility, and become more interested in getting the job done
        (3)   To improve a supervisor's performance by relieving him of routine jobs and giving him more time for *executive functions* (planning, organizing, controlling, etc.) which cannot be delegated

2. <u>To Whom to Delegate</u>
    People with abilities not being used. Selection should be based on ability, not on favoritism.

REPORTS

<u>Definition</u>
    A report is an orderly presentation of factual information directed to a specific reader for a specific purpose.

<u>Purpose</u>
    The general purpose of a report is to bring to the reader useful and factual information about a condition or a problem. Some specific purposes of a report may be:

1. To enable the reader to appraise the efficiency or effectiveness of a person or an operation
2. To provide a basis for establishing standards
3. To reflect the results of expenditures of time, effort, and money
4. To provide a basis for developing or altering programs

Types

1. Information Report - Contains facts arranged in sequence
2. Summary (Examination) Report - Contains facts plus an analysis or discussion of the significance of the facts. Analysis may give advantages and disadvantages or give qualitative and quantitative comparisons
3. Recommendation Report - Contains facts, analysis, and conclusion logically drawn from the facts and analysis, plus a recommendation based upon the facts, analysis, and conclusions

Factors to Consider Before Writing Report

1. Why write the report - The purpose of the report should be clearly defined.
2. Who will read the report - What level of language should be used? Will the reader understand professional or technical language?
3. What should be said - What does the reader need or want to know about the subject?
4. How should it be said - Should the subject be presented tactfully? Convincingly? In a stimulating manner?

Preparatory Steps

1. Assemble the facts - Find out who, why, what, where, when, and how.
2. Organize the facts - Eliminate unnecessary information.
3. Prepare an outline - Check for orderliness, logical sequence.
4. Prepare a draft - Check for correctness, clearness, completeness, conciseness, and tone.
5. Prepare it in final form - Check for grammar, punctuation, appearance.

Outline For a Recommendation Report
Is the report:

1. Correct in information, grammar, and tone?
2. Clear?
3. Complete?
4. Concise?
5. Timely?
6. Worth its cost?

Will the report accomplish its purpose?

MANAGEMENT CONTROLS

1. Control
   What is control? What is controlled? Who controls?

   The essence of control is action which adjusts operations to predetermined standards, and its basis is information in the hands of managers. Control is checking to determine whether plans are being observed and suitable progress toward stated objectives is being made, and action is taken, if necessary, to correct deviations.

We have a ready-made model for this concept of control in the automatic systems which are widely used for process control in the chemical and petroleum industries. A process control system works this way. Suppose, for example, it is desired to maintain a constant rate of flow of oil through a pipe at a predetermined or set-point value. A signal, whose strength represents the rate of flow, can be produced in a measuring device and transmitted to a control mechanism. The control mechanism, when it detects any deviation of the actual from the set-point signal, will reposition the value regulating flow rate.

2. Basis For Control
A process control mechanism thus acts to adjust operations to predetermined standards and does so on the basis of information it receives. In a parallel way, information reaching a manager gives him the opportunity for corrective action and is his basis for control. He cannot exercise control without such information, and he cannot do a complete job of managing without controlling.

3. Policy
What is policy?

Policy is simply a statement of an organization's intention to act in certain ways when specified types of circumstances arise. It represents a general decision, predetermined and expressed as a principle or rule, establishing a normal pattern of conduct for dealing with given types of business events - usually recurrent. A statement is therefore useful in economizing the time of managers and in assisting them to discharge their responsibilities equitably and consistently.

Policy is not a means of control, but policy does generate the need for control.

Adherence to policies is not guaranteed nor can it be taken on faith. It has to be verified. Without verification, there is no basis for control. Policy and procedures, although closely related and interdependent to a certain extent, are not synonymous. A policy may be adopted, for example, to maintain a materials inventory not to exceed one million dollars. A procedure for inventory control would interpret that policy and convert it into methods for keeping within that limit, with consideration, too, of possible but foreseeable expedient deviation.

4. Procedure
What is procedure?

A procedure specifically prescribes:

    a. What work is to be performed by the various participants
    b. Who are the respective participants
    c. When and where the various steps in the different processes are to be performed
    d. The sequence of operations that will insure uniform handling of recurring transactions
    e. The *paper* that is involved, its origin, transition, and disposition

Necessary appurtenances to a procedure are:

    a. Detailed organizational chart

b. Flow charts
c. Exhibits of forms, all presented in close proximity to the text of the procedure

5. Basis of Control - Information in the Hands of Managers
    If the basis of control is information in the hands of managers, then reporting is elevated to a level of very considerable importance.

    Types of reporting may include:

    a. Special reports and routine reports
    b. Written, oral, and graphic reports
    c. Staff meetings
    d. Conferences
    e. Television screens
    f. Non-receipt of information, as where management is by exception
    g. Any other means whereby information is transmitted to a manager as a basis for control action

FRAMEWORK OF MANAGEMENT

Elements

1. Policy - It has to be verified, controlled.

2. Organization - is part of the giving of an assignment. The organizational chart gives to each individual in his title, a first approximation of the nature of his assignment and orients him as being accountable to a certain individual. Organization is not in a true sense a means of control. Control is checking to ascertain whether the assignment is executed as intended and acting on the basis of that information.

3. Budgets - perform three functions:

    a. They present the objectives, plans, and programs of the organization in financial terms.
    b. They report the progress of actual performance against these predetermined objectives, plans, and programs.
    c. Like organizational charts, delegations of authority, procedures and job descriptions, they define the assignments which have flowed from the Chief Executive. Budgets are a means of control in the respect that they report progress of actual performance against the program. They provide information which enables managers to take action directed toward bringing actual results into conformity with the program.

4. Internal Check - provides in practice for the principle that the same person should not have responsibility for all phases of a transaction. This makes it clearly an aspect of organization rather than of control. Internal Check is static, or built-in.

5. Plans, Programs, Objectives
    People must know what they are trying to do. Objectives fulfill this need. Without them, people may work industriously and yet, working aimlessly, accomplish little.

Plans and Programs complement Objectives, since they propose how and according to what time schedule the objectives are to be reached.

6. Delegations of Authority

Among the ways we have for supplementing the titles and lines of authority of an organizational chart are delegations of authority. Delegations of authority clarify the extent of authority of individuals and in that way serve to define assignments. That they are not means of control is apparent from the very fact that wherever there has been a delegation of authority, the need for control increases. This could hardly be expected to happen if delegations of authority were themselves means of control.

Manager's Responsibility

Control becomes necessary whenever a manager delegates authority to a subordinate because he cannot delegate and then simply sit back and forget all about it. A manager's accountability to his own superior has not diminished one whit as a result of delegating part of his authority to a subordinate. The manager must exercise control over actions taken under the authority so delegated. That means checking serves as a basis for possible corrective action.

Objectives, plans, programs, organizational charts, and other elements of the managerial system are not fruitfully regarded as either controls or means of control. They are pre-established standards or models of performance to which operations are adjusted by the exercise of management control. These standards or models of performance are dynamic in character for they are constantly altered, modified, or revised. Policies, organizational set-up, procedures, delegations, etc. are constantly altered but, like objectives and plans, they remain in force until they are either abandoned or revised. All of the elements (or standards or models of performance), objectives, plans and prpgrams, policies, organization, etc. can be regarded as a *framework of management*.

Control Techniques

Examples of control techniques:
1. Compare against established standards
2. Compare with a similar operation
3. Compare with past operations
4. Compare with predictions of accomplishment

Where Forecasts Fit

Control is after-the-fact while forecasts are before. Forecasts and projections are important for setting objectives and formulating plans.

Information for aiming and planning does not have to before-the-fact. It may be an after-the-fact analysis proving that a certain policy has been impolitic in its effect on the relation of the company or department with customer, employee, taxpayer, or stockholder; or that a certain plan is no longer practical, or that a certain procedure is unworkable.

The prescription here certainly would not be in control (in these cases, control would simply bring operations into conformity with obsolete standards) but the establishment of new standards, a new policy, a new plan, and a new procedure to be controlled too.

Information is, of course, the basis for all communication in addition to furnishing evidence to management of the need for reconstructing the framework of management.

PROBLEM SOLVING

The accepted concept in modern management for problem solving is the utilization of the following steps:

1. Identify the problem
2. Gather data
3. List possible solutions
4. Test possible solutions
5. Select the best solution
6. Put the solution into actual practice

Occasions might arise where you would have to apply the second step of gathering data before completing the first step.

You might also find that it will be necessary to work on several steps at the same time.

1. Identify the Problem

    Your first step is to define as precisely as possible the problem to be solved. While this may sound easy, it is often the most difficult part of the process.

    It has been said of problem solving that you are halfway to the solution when you can write out a clear statement of the problem itself.

    Our job now is to get below the surface manifestations of the trouble and pinpoint the problem. This is usually accomplished by a logical analysis, by going from the general to the particular; from the obvious to the not-so-obvious cause.
    Let us say that production is behind schedule. WHY? Absenteeism is high. Now, is absenteeism the basic problem to be tackled, or is it merely a symptom of low morale among the workforce? Under these circumstances, you may decide that production is not the problem; the problem is *employee morale*.

    In trying to define the problem, remember there is seldom one simple reason why production is lagging, or reports are late, etc.

    Analysis usually leads to the discovery that an apparent problem is really made up of several subproblems which must be attacked separately.

    Another way is to limit the problem, and thereby ease the task of finding a solution, and concentrate on the elements which are within the scope of your control.

    When you have gone this far, write out a tentative statement of the problem to be solved.

2. Gather Data

In the second step, you must set out to collect all the information that might have a bearing on the problem. Do not settle for an assumption when reasonable fact and figures are available.

If you merely go through the motions of problem-solving, you will probably shortcut the information-gathering step. Therefore, do not stack the evidence by confining your research to your own preconceived ideas.

As you collect facts, organize them in some form that helps you make sense of them and spot possible relationships between them. For example: Plotting cost per unit figures on a graph can be more meaningful than a long column of figures.

Evaluate each item as you go along. Is the source material: absolutely reliable, probably reliable, or not to be trusted.

One of the best methods for gathering data is to go out and look the situation over carefully. Talk to the people on the job who are most affected by this problem.

Always keep in mind that a primary source is usually better than a secondary source of information.

3. List Possible Solutions

This is the creative thinking step of problem solving. This is a good time to bring into play whatever techniques of group dynamics the agency or bureau might have developed for a joint attack on problems.

Now the important thing for you to do is: Keep an open mind. Let your imagination roam freely over the facts you have collected. Jot down every possible solution that occurs to you. Resist the temptation to evaluate various proposals as you go along. List seemingly absurd ideas along with more plausible ones. The more possibilities you list during this step, the less risk you will run of settling for merely a workable, rather than the best, solution.

Keep studying the data as long as there seems to be any chance of deriving additional - ideas, solutions, explanations, or patterns from it.

4. Test Possible Solutions

Now you begin to evaluate the possible solutions. Take pains to be objective. Up to this point, you have suspended judgment but you might be tempted to select a solution you secretly favored all along and proclaim it as the best of the lot.

The secret of objectivity in this phase is to test the possible solutions separately, measuring each against a common yardstick. To make this yardstick try to enumerate as many specific criteria as you can think of. Criteria are best phrased as questions which you ask of each possible solution. They can be drawn from these general categories:

Suitability   -   Will this solution do the job?
                    Will it solve the problem completely or partially?

Is it a permanent or a stopgap solution?

Feasibility   -   Will this plan work in actual practice?
Can we afford this approach?
How much will it cost?

Acceptability -   Will the boss go along with the changes required in the plan?
Are we trying to drive a tack with a sledge hammer?

5. <u>Select the Best Solution</u>

This is the area of executive decision.

Occasionally, one clearly superior solution will stand out at the conclusion of the testing process. But often it is not that simple. You may find that no one solution has come through all the tests with flying colors.

You may also find that a proposal, which flunked miserably on one of the essential tests, racked up a very high score on others.

The best solution frequently will turn out to be a combination.

Try to arrange a marriage that will bring together the strong points of one possible solution with the particular virtues of another. The more skill and imagination that you apply, the greater is the likelihood that you will come out with a solution that is not merely adequate and workable, but is the best possible under the circumstances.

6. <u>Put the Solution Into Actual Practice</u>
As every executive knows, a plan which works perfectly on paper may develop all sorts of bugs when put into actual practice.

Problem-solving does not stop with selecting the solution which looks best in theory. The next step is to put the chosen solution into action and watch the results. The results may point towards modifications.

If the problem disappears when you put your solution into effect, you know you have the right solution.

If it does not disappear, even after you have adjusted your plan to cover unforeseen difficulties that turned up in practice, work your way back through the problem-solving solutions.

Would one of them have worked better?
Did you overlook some vital piece of data which would have given you a different slant on the whole situation? Did you apply all necessary criteria in testing solutions? If no light dawns after this much rechecking, it is a pretty good bet that you defined the problem incorrectly in the first place.

You came up with the wrong solution because you tackled the wrong problem.

Thus, step six may become step one of a new problem-solving cycle.

COMMUNICATION

1. <u>What is Communication</u>?
    We communicate through writing, speaking, action or inaction. In speaking to people face-to-face, there is opportunity to judge reactions and to adjust the message. This makes the supervisory chain one of the most, and in many instances the most, important channels of communication.

    In an organization, communication means keeping employees informed about the organization's objectives, policies, problems, and progress. Communication is the free interchange of information, ideas, and desirable attitudes between and among employees and between employees and management.

2. <u>Why is Communication Needed</u>?
    a. People have certain social needs
    b. Good communication is essential in meeting those social needs
    c. While people have similar basic needs, at the same time they differ from each other
    d. Communication must be adapted to these individual differences

    An employee cannot do his best work unless he knows why he is doing it. If he has the feeling that he is being kept in the dark about what is going on, his enthusiasm and productivity suffer.

    Effective communication is needed in an organization so that employees will understand what the organization is trying to accomplish; and how the work of one unit contributes to or affects the work of other units in the organization and other organizations.

3. <u>How is Communication Achieved?</u>
    Communication flows downward, upward, sideways.

    a. Communication may come from top management down to employees. This is <u>downward communication</u>.

        Some means of downward communication are:
        (1) Training (orientation, job instruction, supervision, public relations, etc.)
        (2) Conferences
        (3) Staff meetings
        (4) Policy statements
        (5) Bulletins
        (6) Newsletters
        (7) Memoranda
        (8) Circulation of important letters

        In downward communication, it is important that employees be informed in advance of changes that will affect them.

    b. Communications should also be developed so that the ideas, suggestions, and knowledge of employees will flow <u>upward</u> to top management.

Some means of upward communication are:
(1)   Personal discussion conferences
(2)   Committees
(3)   Memoranda
(4)   Employees suggestion program
(5)   Questionnaires to be filled in giving comments and suggestions about proposed actions that will affect field operations

Upward communication requires that management be willing to listen, to accept, and to make changes when good ideas are present. Upward communication succeeds when there is no fear of punishment for speaking out or lack of interest at the top. Employees will share their knowledge and ideas with management when interest is shown and recognition is given.

   c.   The *advantages* of downward communication:
   (1)   It enables the passing down of orders, policies, and plans necessary to the continued operation of the station.
   (2)   By making information available, it diminishes the fears and suspicions which result from misinformation and misunderstanding.
   (3)   It fosters the pride people want to have in their work when they are told of good work.
   (4)   It improves the morale and stature of the individual to be *in the know.*
   (5)   It helps employees to understand, accept, and cooperate with changes when they know about them in advance.

   d.   The *advantages* of upward communication:
   (1)   It enables the passing upward of information, attitudes, and feelings.
   (2)   It makes it easier to find out how ready people are to receive downward communication.
   (3)   It reveals the degree to which the downward communication is understood and accepted.
   (4)   It helps to satisfy the basic *social* needs.
   (5)   It stimulates employees to participate in the operation of their organization.
   (6)   It encourages employees to contribute ideas for improving the efficiency and economy of operations.
   (7)   It helps to solve problem situations before they reach the explosion point.

4.   Why Does Communication Fail?
   a.   The technical difficulties of conveying information clearly
   b.   The emotional content of communication which prevents complete transmission
   c.   The fact that there is a difference between what management needs to say, what it wants to say, and what it does say
   d.   The fact that there is a difference between what employees would like to say, what they think is profitable or safe to say, and what they do say

5.   How to Improve Communication.
   As a supervisor, you are a key figure in communication. To improve as a communicator, you should:
   a.   Know - Knowing your subordinates will help you to recognize and work with individual differences.

b. <u>Like</u> - If you like those who work for you and those for whom you work, this will foster the kind of friendly, warm, work atmosphere that will facilitate communication.

c. <u>Trust</u> - Showing a sincere desire to communicate will help to develop the mutual trust and confidence which are essential to the free flow of communication.

d. <u>Tell</u> - Tell your subordinates and superiors *what's doing*. Tell your subordinates *why* as well as *how*.

e. <u>Listen</u> - By listening, you help others to talk and you create good listeners. Don't forget that listening implies action.

f. <u>Stimulate</u> - Communication has to be stimulated and encouraged. Be receptive to ideas and suggestions and motivate your people so that each member of the team identifies himself with the job at hand.

g. <u>Consult</u> - The most effective way of consulting is to let your people participate, insofar as possible, in developing determinations which affect them or their work.

6. <u>How to Determine Whether You are Getting Across</u>.
   a. Check to see that communication is received and understood
   b. Judge this understanding by actions rather than words
   c. Adapt or vary communication, when necessary
   d. Remember that good communication cannot cure all problems

7. <u>The Key Attitude</u>.
   Try to see things from the other person's point of view. By doing this, you help to develop the permissive atmosphere and the shared confidence and understanding which are essential to effective two-way communication.

   Communication is a two-way process.
   a. The basic purpose of any communication is to get action.
   b. The only way to get action is through acceptance.
   c. In order to get acceptance, communication must be humanly satisfying as well as technically efficient.

HOW ORDERS AND INSTRUCTIONS SHOULD BE GIVEN

<u>Characteristics of Good Orders and Instructions</u>

1. <u>Clear</u>
   Orders should be definite as to
   - <u>What</u> is to be done
   - <u>Who</u> is to do it
   - <u>When</u> it is to be done
   - <u>Where</u> it is to be done
   - <u>How</u> it is to be done

2. <u>Concise</u>
   Avoid wordiness. Orders should be brief and to the point.

3. <u>Timely</u>
   Instructions and orders should be sent out at the proper time and not too long in advance of expected performance.

4. Possibility of Performance
   Orders should be feasible:
   a. Investigate before giving orders
   b. Consult those who are to carry out instructions before formulating and issuing them

5. Properly Directed
   Give the orders to the people concerned. Do not send orders to people who are not concerned. People who continually receive instructions that are not applicable to them get in the habit of neglecting instructions generally.

6. Reviewed Before Issuance
   Orders should be reviewed before issuance:
   a. Test them by putting yourself in the position of the recipient
   b. If they involve new procedures, have the persons who are to do the work review them for suggestions

7. Reviewed After Issuance
   Persons who receive orders should be allowed to raise questions and to point out unforeseen consequences of orders.

8. Coordinated
   Orders should be coordinated so that work runs smoothly.

9. Courteous
   Make a request rather than a demand. There is no need to continually call attention to the fact that you are the boss.

10. Recognizable as an Order
    Be sure that the order is recognizable as such.

11. Complete
    Be sure recipient has knowledge and experience sufficient to carry out order. Give illustrations and examples.

A DEPARTMENTAL PERSONNEL OFFICE IS RESPONSIBLE FOR THE FOLLOWING FUNCTIONS

1. Policy
2. Personnel Programs
3. Recruitment and Placement
4. Position Classification
5. Salary and Wage Administration
6. Employee Performance Standards and Evaluation
7. Employee Relations
8. Disciplinary Actions and Separations
9. Health and Safety
10. Staff Training and Development
11. Personnel Records, Procedures, and Reports
12. Employee Services
13. Personnel Research

SUPERVISION

Leadership

All leadership is based essentially on authority. This comes from two sources: it is received from higher management or it is earned by the supervisor through his methods of supervision. Although effective leadership has always depended upon the leader's using his authority in such a way as to appeal successfully to the motives of the people supervised, the conditions for making this appeal are continually changing. The key to today's problem of leadership is flexibility and resourcefulness on the part of the leader in meeting changes in conditions as they occur.

Three basic approaches to leadership are generally recognized:

1. The Authoritarian Approach
    a. The methods and techniques used in this approach emphasize the *I* in leadership and depend primarily on the formal authority of the leader. This authority is sometimes exercised in a hardboiled manner and sometimes in a benevolent manner, but in either case the dominating role of the leader is reflected in the thinking, planning, and decisions of the group.
    b. Group results are to a large degree dependent on close supervision by the leader. Usually, the individuals in the group will not show a high degree of initiative or acceptance of responsibility and their capacity to grow and develop probably will not be fully utilized. The group may react with resentment or submission, depending upon the manner and skill of the leader in using his authority
    c. This approach develops as a natural outgrowth of the authority that goes with the leader's job and his feeling of sole responsibility for getting the job done. It is relatively easy to use and does not require much resourcefulness.
    d. The use of this approach is effective in times of emergencies, in meeting close deadlines as a final resort, in settling some issues, in disciplinary matters, and with dependent individuals and groups.

2. The Laissez-Faire or *Let 'em Alone* Approach
    a. This approach generally is characterized by an avoidance of leadership responsibility by the leader. The activities of the group depend largely on the choice of its members rather than the leader.
    b. Group results probably will be poor. Generally, there will be disagreements over petty things, bickering, and confusion. Except for a few aggressive people, individuals will not show much initiative and growth and development will be retarded. There may be a tendency for informal leaders to take over leadership of the group.
    c. This approach frequently results from the leader's dislike of responsibility, from his lack of confidence, from failure of other methods to work, from disappointment or criticism. It is usually the easiest of the three to use and requires both understanding and resourcefulness on the part of the leader.
    d. This approach is occasionally useful and effective, particularly in forcing dependent individuals or groups to rely on themselves, to give someone a chance to save face by clearing his own difficulties, or when action should be delayed temporarily for good cause.

3. The Democratic Approach
   a. The methods and techniques used in this approach emphasize the *we* in leadership and build up the responsibility of the group to attain its objectives. Reliance is placed largely on the earned authority of the leader.
   b. Group results are likely to be good because most of the job motives of the people will be satisfied. Cooperation and teamwork, initiative, acceptance of responsibility, and the individual's capacity for growth probably will show a high degree of development.
   c. This approach grows out of a desire or necessity of the leader to find ways to appeal effectively to the motivation of his group. It is the best approach to build up inside the person a strong desire to cooperate and apply himself to the job.
   It is the most difficult to develop, and requires both understanding and resourcefulness on the part of the leader.
   d. The value of this approach increases over a long period where sustained efficiency and development of people are important. It may not be fully effective in all situations, however, particularly when there is not sufficient time to use it properly or where quick decisions must be made.

All three approaches are used by most leaders and have a place in supervising people. The extent of their use varies with individual leaders, with some using one approach predominantly. The leader who uses these three approaches, and varies their use with time and circumstance, is probably the most effective. Leadership which is used predominantly with a democratic approach requires more resourcefulness on the part of the leader but offers the greatest possibilities in terms of teamwork and cooperation.

The one best way of developing democratic leadership is to provide a real sense of participation on the part of the group, since this satisfies most of the chief job motives. Although there are many ways of providing participation, consulting as frequently as possible with individuals and groups on things that affect them seems to offer the most in building cooperation and responsibility. Consultation takes different forms, but it is most constructive when people feel they are actually helping in finding the answers to the problems on the job.

There are some requirements of leaders in respect to human relations which should be considered in their selection and development. Generally, the leader should be interested in working with other people, emotionally stable, self-confident, and sensitive to the reactions of others. In addition, his viewpoint should be one of getting the job done through people who work cooperatively in response to his leadership. He should have a knowledge of individual and group behavior, but, most important of all, he should work to combine all of these requirements into a definite, practical skill in leadership.

Nine Points of Contrast Between *Boss* and *Leader*

1. The boss drives his men; the leader coaches them.
2. The boss depends on authority; the leader on good will.
3. The boss inspires fear; the leader inspires enthusiasm.
4. The boss says J; the leader says *We*.
5. The boss says *Get here on time;* the leader gets there ahead of time.
6. The boss fixes the blame for the breakdown; the leader fixes the breakdown.
7. The boss knows how it is done; the leader shows how.
8. The boss makes work a drudgery; the leader makes work a game.
9. The boss says *Go*; the leader says *Let's go.*

EMPLOYEE MORALE

Employee morale is the way employees feel about each other, the organization or unit in which they work, and the work they perform.

Some Ways to Develop and Maintain Good Employee Morale

1. Give adequate credit and praise when due.
2. Recognize importance of all jobs and equalize load with proper assignments, always giving consideration to personality differences and abilities.
3. Welcome suggestions and do not have an *all-wise* attitude. Request employees' assistance in solving problems and use assistants when conducting group meetings on certain subjects.
4. Properly assign responsibilities and give adequate authority for fulfillment of such assignments.
5. Keep employees informed about matters that affect them.
6. Criticize and reprimand employees privately.
7. Be accessible and willing to listen.
8. Be fair.
9. Be alert to detect training possibilities so that you will not miss an opportunity to help each employee do a better job, and if possible with less effort on his part.
10. Set a good example.
11. Apply the golden rule.

Some Indicators of Good Morale
1. Good quality of work
2. Good quantity
3. Good attitude of employees
4. Good discipline
5. Teamwork
6. Good attendance
7. Employee participation

MOTIVATION

Drives

A *drive*, stated simply, is a desire or force which causes a person to do or say certain things. These are some of the most usual drives and some of their identifying characteristics recognizable in people motivated by such drives:

1. Security (desire to provide for the future)
   Always on time for work
   Works for the same employer for many years
   Never takes unnecessary chances Seldom resists doing what he is told

2. Recognition (desire to be rewarded for accomplishment)
   Likes to be asked for his opinion
   Becomes very disturbed when he makes a mistake
   Does things to attract attention

Likes to see his name in print

3. Position (desire to hold certain status in relation to others)
    Boasts about important people he knows
    Wants to be known as a key man
    Likes titles
    Demands respect
    Belongs to clubs, for prestige

4. Accomplishment (desire to get things done)
    Complains when things are held up
    Likes to do things that have tangible results
    Never lies down on the job
    Is proud of turning out good work

5. Companionship (desire to associate with other people)
    Likes to work with others
    Tells stories and jokes
    Indulges in horseplay
    Finds excuses to talk to others on the job

6. Possession (desire to collect and hoard objects)
    Likes to collect things
    Puts his name on things belonging to him
    Insists on the same work location

Supervisors may find that identifying the drives of employees is a helpful step toward motivating them to self-improvement and better job performance. For example: An employee's job performance is below average. His supervisor, having previously determined that the employee is motivated by a drive for security, suggests that taking training courses will help the employee to improve, advance, and earn more money. Since earning more money can be a step toward greater security, the employee's drive for security would motivate him to take the training suggested by the supervisor. In essence, this is the process of charting an employee's future course by using his motivating drives to positive advantage.

EMPLOYEE PARTICIPATION

What is Participation?

Employee participation is the employee's giving freely of his time, skill and knowledge to an extent which cannot be obtained by demand.

Why is it Important?

The supervisor's responsibility is to get the job done through people. A good supervisor gets the job done through people who work willingly and well. The participation of employees is important because:

1. Employees develop a greater sense of responsibility when they share in working out operating plans and goals.
2. Participation provides greater opportunity and stimulation for employees to learn, and to develop their ability.

3. Participation sometimes provides better solutions to problems because such solutions may combine the experience and knowledge of interested employees who want the solutions to work.
4. An employee or group may offer a solution which the supervisor might hesitate to make for fear of demanding too much.
5. Since the group wants to make the solution work, they exert *pressure* in a constructive way on each other.
6. Participation usually results in reducing the need for close supervision.

How May Supervisors Obtain It?

Participation is encouraged when employees feel that they share some responsibility for the work and that their ideas are sincerely wanted and valued. Some ways of obtaining employee participation are:

1. Conduct orientation programs for new employees to inform them about the organization and their rights and responsibilities as employees.
2. Explain the aims and objectives of the agency. On a continuing basis, be sure that the employees know what these aims and objectives are.
3. Share job successes and responsibilities and give credit for success.
4. Consult with employees, both as individuals and in groups, about things that affect them.
5. Encourage suggestions for job improvements. Help employees to develop good suggestions. The suggestions can bring them recognition. The city's suggestion program offers additional encouragement through cash awards.

The supervisor who encourages employee participation is not surrendering his authority. He must still make decisions and initiate action, and he must continue to be ultimately responsible for the work of those he supervises. But, through employee participation, he is helping his group to develop greater ability and a sense of responsibility while getting the job done faster and better.

STEPS IN HANDLING A GRIEVANCE

1. Get the facts
   a. Listen sympathetically.
   b. Let him talk himself out.
   c. Get his story straight.
   d. Get his point of view.
   e. Don't argue with him.
   f. Give him plenty of time.
   g. Conduct the interview privately.
   h. Don't try to shift the blame or pass the buck.

2. Consider the facts
   a. Consider the employee's viewpoint.
   b. How will the decision affect similar cases.
   c. Consider each decision as a possible precedent.
   d. Avoid snap judgments - don't jump to conclusions.

3. <u>Make or get a decision</u>
   a. Frame an effective counter-proposal.
   b. Make sure it is fair to all.
   c. Have confidence in your judgment.
   d. Be sure you can substantiate your decision.

4. <u>Notify the employee of your decision</u>
   Be sure he is told; try to convince him that the decision is fair and just.

5. <u>Take action when needed and if within your authority</u>
   Otherwise, tell employee that the matter will be called to the attention of the proper person or that nothing can be done, and why it cannot.

6. <u>Follow through</u> to see that the desired result is achieved.

7. <u>Record key facts</u> concerning the complaint and the action taken.

8. <u>Leave the way open to him to appeal your decision</u> to a higher authority.

9. <u>Report all grievances to your superior</u>, whether they are appealed or not.

DISCIPLINE

Discipline is training that develops self-control, orderly conduct, and efficiency.

To discipline does not necessarily mean to punish.

To discipline does mean to train, to regulate, and to govern conduct.

<u>The Disciplinary Interview</u>

Most employees sincerely want to do what is expected of them. In other words, they are self-disciplined. Some employees, however, fail to observe established rules and standards, and disciplinary action by the supervisor is required.

The primary purpose of disciplinary action is to improve conduct without creating dissatisfaction, bitterness, or resentment in the process.

Constructive disciplinary action is more concerned with causes and explanations of breaches of conduct than with punishment. The disciplinary interview is held to get at the causes of apparent misbehavior and to motivate better performance in the future.

It is important that the interview be kept on as impersonal a basis as possible. If the supervisor lets the interview descend to the plane of an argument, it loses its effectiveness.

<u>Planning the Interview</u>

Get all pertinent facts concerning the situation so that you can talk in specific terms to the employee.

Review the employee's record, appraisal ratings, etc.

Consider what you know about the temperament of the employee. Consider your attitude toward the employee. Remember that the primary requisite of disciplinary action is fairness.

Don't enter upon the interview when angry.

Schedule the interview for a place which is private and out of hearing of others.

Conducting the Interview

1. Make an effort to establish accord.

2. Question the employee about the apparent breach of discipline. Be sure that the question is not so worded as to be itself an accusation.

3. Give the employee a chance to tell his side of the story. Give him ample opportunity to talk.

4. Use understanding-listening except where it is necessary to ask a question or to point out some details of which the employee may not be aware. If the employee misrepresents facts, make a plain, accurate statement of the facts, but don't argue and don't engage in personal controversy.

5. Listen and try to understand the reasons for the employee's (mis)conduct. First of all, don't assume that there has been a breach of discipline. Evaluate the employee's reasons for his conduct in the light of his opinions and feelings concerning the consistency and reasonableness of the standards which he was expected to follow. Has the supervisor done his part in explaining the reasons for the rules? Was the employee's behavior unintentional or deliberate? Does he think he had real reasons for his actions? What new facts is he telling? Do the facts justify his actions? What causes, other than those mentioned, could have stimulated the behavior?

6. After listening to the employee's version of the situation, and if censure of his actions is warranted, the supervisor should proceed with whatever criticism is justified. Emphasis should be placed on future improvement rather than exclusively on the employee's failure to measure up to expected standards of job conduct.

7. Fit the criticism to the individual. With one employee, a word of correction may be all that is required.

8. Attempt to distinguish between unintentional error and deliberate misbehavior. An error due to ignorance requires training and not censure.

9. Administer criticism in a controlled, even tone of voice, never in anger. Make it clear that you are acting as an agent of the department. In general, criticism should refer to the job or the employee's actions and not to the person. Criticism of the employee's work is not an attack on the individual.

10. Be sure the interview does not destroy the employee's self-confidence. Mention his good qualities and assure him that you feel confident that he can improve his performance.

11. Wherever possible, before the employee leaves the interview, satisfy him that the incident is closed, that nothing more will be said on the subject unless the offense is repeated.

———